GARDEN BIRDS

in Southern Africa

DUNCAN BUTCHART

Published by Struik Nature
(an imprint of Penguin Random House South Africa (Pty) Ltd)
Reg. No. 1953/000441/07
The Estuaries No. 4, Oxbow Crescent (off Century Avenue),
Century City, 7441 South Africa
PO Box 1144, Cape Town, 8000 South Africa

Visit www.penguinrandomhouse.co.za and join the Struik Nature Club
for updates, news, events and special offers.

First published in 2017 by Struik Nature

1 3 5 7 9 10 8 6 4 2

Copyright © in text, 2017: Duncan Butchart
Copyright © in photographs, 2017: Duncan Butchart,
except where listed alongside photograph
Copyright © in illustrations, 2017: Duncan Butchart
Copyright © in maps, 2017: Penguin Random House South Africa (Pty) Ltd
Copyright © in published edition, 2017:
Penguin Random House South Africa (Pty) Ltd

Publisher: Pippa Parker
Managing editor: Helen de Villiers
Editor: Emily Donaldson
Designer: Neil Bester
Proofreader and indexer: Thea Grobbelaar

Reproduction by Hirt & Carter Cape (Pty) Ltd
Printed and bound by C&C Offset Printing Co., Ltd.

All rights reserved. No part of this publication may be reproduced,
stored in a retrieval system, or transmitted, in any form or by any means,
electronic, mechanical, photocopying, recording or otherwise,
without the prior written permission of the copyright owner(s).

Print: 9781775844747
ePub: 9781775844754
ePDF: 9781775844761

Front cover: African Paradise Flycatcher (Don Hunter)
Back cover: (top) Cape Bulbul;
(photo strip, left to right) Common Waxbills (Neil Ebedes);
Cape Sugarbird; Cape White-eye; African Red-eyed Bulbul
Page 1: Malachite Sunbird
Opposite: Spotted Eagle-Owl

CONTENTS

ACKNOWLEDGEMENTS 5

AUTHOR'S NOTE 6

FOREWORD 7

INTRODUCTION 9
Bird-friendly gardening 9
The climate and biomes of southern Africa 11

THE GARDEN 15
Creating garden habitats 15
Providing water 23
Providing food 28
Providing nest sites 33
Dangers facing garden birds 36

THE BIRDS 41
Watching birds 41
Bird anatomy 42
Bird calls 43
Feeding behaviour 44
Breeding behaviour 44
Seasonal migration 47

101 GARDEN BIRDS 49
Bird species 51–151
Extraordinary and unusual garden visitors 152

THE PLANTS 155
Choosing and placing plants 155
50 bird-friendly trees, shrubs and climbers 159
Proteas and other fynbos plants 175
Aloes 176
Decorative plants 178
Grasses 180
Invasive alien plants 181

BIRDS IN BOTANICAL GARDENS 182

USEFUL RESOURCES 186

REFERENCES AND FURTHER READING 187

GLOSSARY 188

INDEXES 189

'Turaco Wood', Nelspruit – the bird-filled garden that the author created and called home for over 20 years.

ACKNOWLEDGEMENTS

To begin with, I would like to thank Pippa Parker and Helen de Villiers of Struik Nature for inviting me to compile this book, and to their colleagues Emily Donaldson (editor) and Neil Bester (designer) for turning my texts and images into such an attractive publication.

Wherever I have set up a home, I have grown indigenous plants and encouraged birds to share the outdoor space. My first attempts at 'bird gardening' took place at my parents' home in Mondeor, south of Johannesburg, in the 1970s, where Black-collared Barbets took occupation of my schoolboy nest boxes and Malachite Sunbirds bathed in sprinkler showers I would set up on hot afternoons; way back then Ken Newman, John Freer and John Ledger were among those who encouraged my interest in birds. Over the years, I have lived alongside Red-throated Wrynecks in Fourways, Green Wood-hoopoes in Parkhurst, Hadeda Ibis in Randpark Ridge, and – for 20 years – with Purple-crested Turacos and African Wood Owls at 'Turaco Wood' in Nelspruit. Presently, and while writing this book, I have been reunited with Malachite Sunbirds that feed and sing outside our windows in the coastal town of Hermanus not far from the very southern tip of the African continent.

My own knowledge of garden birds and plants has grown through the sharing of experiences and observations with friends and family over many years, including David Allan, Tania Anderson, Karen Bullen, John Burrows, Graeme Butchart, Ann Cameron, Kat Cameron, James Culverwell, Ian Davidson, Greg Davies, Billy Doepel, Bonnie and Russel Friedman, Pete Hancock, Lex Hes, Marie Holstensson, Laura-Ann Keates, Peta Kennedy, Alastair Kilpin, Emilia Knight, Peter Lawson, Geoff Lockwood, Peter Mundy, Kevin Mansfield, Hugh Marshall, Tamar Mason, Steven Piper, Ingrid Meyer, Drew Paterson, Beth Peterson, Diane Peterson, Shelagh Peterson, Christine Read, Wendy Sippel, Derek Solomon, Peter Steyn, Warwick Tarboton, Greg Theron and Leigh Voigt. Thanks to you all!

Several people have contributed photographs or information to this book, and I am grateful to the following friends and fellow enthusiasts of wild gardens: Tim Cockcroft, James Culverwell, Neil Ebedes, Ryan and Glenice Ebedes, Pete Hancock, Trevor Hardaker, Jonathan Haw, Malcolm Hepplewhite, Vicki Hill, Don Hunter, Andrew Keys, Chris Krog, and Warwick and Michéle Tarboton. In addition, I am grateful to Mark Anderson of BirdLife South Africa for agreeing to write the Foreword.

Finally, thanks to my wife Tracey and daughter Lily for sharing so many wonderful experiences with garden birds, and for inspiring me to compile this book.

AUTHOR'S NOTE

By and large, birds are terrified of people, and for good reason: we've been hunting and killing every imaginable kind of bird, in unimaginable numbers, for thousands of years. Our earliest ancestors must have obtained a fair amount of their protein from birds, and we currently consume 'game birds', albeit in domesticated form, in astronomical numbers. It is estimated that at least five million migratory birds are shot by Mediterranean hunters every year as they move from Europe to Africa, and vast numbers of wild birds are still captured and eaten in many countries. Whether bearing slingshot, arrow or gun, humans are fearsome and highly efficient predators, and birds regard each and every one of us as a hunter.

Given this relationship, it is rather strange that so many of us derive such pleasure from watching these winged creatures that are so wary and usually cannot get away from us quickly enough. Then again, perhaps it is the very evasiveness of birds that makes them so appealing for us to search for, watch and photograph – a return to the tracking and hunting instincts that are not so very distant in our past, if they have been lost at all.

When we do have an encounter with a wild bird that shows little or no fear of us, there is often a sense of great satisfaction, even intimacy, in the moment. We like to think that the bird is aware that we pose it no danger; that it knows that we just wish to see it go about its own life unmolested by humans.

This desire to have birds accept us as harmless observers may be a subconscious force behind the idea of gardening for birds. If we create a place where birds can safely forage, drink, bathe and even raise their families, then we are making a small atonement for the damage our species has done – and continues to do – to the natural world.

Ray Xmas 2017

FOREWORD

Birds are everywhere – in suburban gardens, in tiny gardens in dense housing estates, and even in downtown concrete jungles. We all awaken to the beautiful sound of calling birds, yet we often forget to appreciate the pleasure it brings to be surrounded by birds. Although granted, the Hadeda Ibises can be a bit irritating!

One cannot miss them, whether it is a Cape Robin-chat singing at dawn, a Little Swift flying to its nest below a ledge on an office block, or a Cape Wagtail walking down the sidewalk looking for tasty tidbits. The birds around us are a constant reminder of the Earth's magnificent biodiversity and the resilience of many animals to adapt to a changing world.

The birds in one's garden provide opportunities for observation, for education, and even for conservation. Every gardener can be a citizen scientist by documenting interesting behaviour, collecting breeding information, or keeping an atlas card. Birds in one's garden can be used to introduce children to the natural world, and this could be the initial stimulus that ultimately results in them one day becoming famous scientists: our children kept a monthly list of the birds in our garden in Kimberley, and we used this to teach them about migration (in months when migratory birds were absent, they asked why this was so), and about geography (we showed them on a map the places where intra-African migrants and Palearctic migrants spend the austral winter).

As the vastness of the Earth's natural world is shrinking, urban environments, including suburban gardens, are becoming increasingly important for the conservation of biodiversity. Whether it be dragonflies at the constructed pond, geckos living under the woodpile, or robin-chats and white-eyes nesting in the shrub thicket, gardens play a small, yet important, role in protecting our heritage.

One of the simplest, yet most satisfying, pastimes is to create a bird-friendly garden. Indigenous plants, a bird feeder, a birdbath, and a sisal nesting log are small ways in which we can attract birds to our gardens. Provide these invitations and they will arrive; that's a guarantee! The satisfaction of watching a weaver splashing in the birdbath, finding a nest in the indigenous creeper, observing a hoopoe feeding its recently fledged young, makes gardening for birds greatly worthwhile.

Duncan Butchart is to be commended on the production of this immensely informative and beautifully illustrated book. He has been a friend, mainly through our common interest in vultures (not typical garden birds!), for about 25 years. Duncan is a very talented artist, photographer, writer and natural historian. He is extremely well qualified to write this book.

It is perhaps fitting that, 50 years after Ken Newman published *Garden Birds of South Africa*, we have another book on the subject. During this half-century, our knowledge of southern African birds has progressed in leaps and bounds, and this book provides up-to-date information on garden birds and recommendations on how to attract them to gardens.

One of my greatest pleasures over the years has been to lie in bed on spring and summer mornings, listening to the dawn chorus. I not only try to identify the singing birds, but also to interpret the contexts in which they are calling. Are they defending a territory or seeking a mate? Most importantly, the cacophony of bird sound in the morning makes me think of a silent dawn. It is unthinkable that, unless we conserve our birds, future generations could wake to a morning without the chatter of birds. We can contribute to the conservation of birds and our natural heritage by ensuring that our gardens are bird-friendly. This book will be the encouragement that will result in many people gardening for birds.

Mark D. Anderson
Chief Executive Officer
BirdLife South Africa

The White-browed Robin-chat can become bold and confiding when feeding opportunities are provided. This is the lowveld counterpart of the more widespread Cape Robin-chat.

INTRODUCTION

Birds will be attracted to your garden if you provide them with the foods they have evolved to eat and the sorts of habitat to which they are adapted. To achieve this, you need a good understanding of the climate and natural vegetation of the region in which you live.

BIRD-FRIENDLY GARDENING

Most of us like to keep a tidy home, and this orderly behaviour generally extends into our gardens too. Lawns are mowed, fallen leaves are swept up, edges are clipped and dead branches are sawn off trees. If invertebrates or fungi attack our plants, we find ways to deal with them. This is all very well if you want a conventional manicured garden, but it is not the best way to encourage the maximum variety of bird species and facilitate the development of a healthy food web.

Many readers of this book will own a small piece of land on which their home is built and will have created a garden space of some kind. We cannot replace the extensive grasslands, renosterveld and coastal forests that have disappeared with ever-increasing agriculture and the spread of suburbia in recent times, but urban dwellers *can* create and maintain habitats that provide birds and other organisms with a home. In the best-case scenario we can retain or extend natural habitats within our gardens.

Not everyone has the budget or opportunity to make modifications to their outdoor living spaces, but even the propagation of a few carefully selected plants and the provision of a simple bird-feeding table or birdbath will attract a good variety of birds. Many South Africans are now living on communal estates, up-market versions of which are sometimes associated with a golf course or parkland, typically overseen and maintained by teams of landscapers. With enthusiasm and knowledge it's possible to encourage better ecological practices on these estates, engaging neighbours and using social media to excite and inform one's community and the wider world.

Birds are probably the most conspicuous and lively of all animals. Some are highly sensitive and survive only in the most pristine environments, but many are adaptable and confiding and live alongside us in towns and cities. A great many people get turned on to birding by seeing birds close-up, outside their windows, sometimes enjoying food that has been specially provided. This is often the first step

Mature trees around the house provide the opportunity for close encounters with garden birds. Nelspruit, Mpumalanga

in appreciating nature as a whole and being part of a greater movement to conserve biodiversity. In some cases, it might also be the first step in a lifelong journey that can take you around the world, seeking out different, wonderful birds in distant countries.

South Africa is a big country, 1.2 million km^2 in area, but here, as is the case elsewhere, wild nature is retreating in the face of an expanding human population. Agriculture, mining, roads and urbanisation have fragmented the landscape, endangering populations of specialised animals and plants, but creating opportunities for adaptable generalist species, including non-native invaders, which often flourish in the company of humankind.

It goes without saying that gardens adjacent to natural habitats will be visited by a greater variety of birds than those deep within suburbia. Nevertheless, the more varied the space around your house, the more varied will be the birds that are attracted. By providing indigenous plants and various feeding niches for wildlife, you can play a vital role in extending the natural habitat and maintaining natural ecological processes, and the more people doing this within your suburb or town, the greater will be the variety of birds seen.

Of course, not everyone has the inclination to turn their garden over to nature, so this book offers a variety of approaches and ideas from which you can pick and choose. Almost any action to encourage birds into your garden will have benefits, but the objective is to make these interventions sustainable. Care must be taken not to allow the spread of invasive plants (the fruits of which many birds relish) or to provide bulk food that can create unnaturally high populations of certain bird species to the detriment of others.

In establishing a more bird-friendly space, the most important thing is to take account of the vegetation zone or biome in which you live. Johannesburg and other parts of the highveld often experience spells of extremely cold winter weather, with severe frost that subtropical or coastal plants

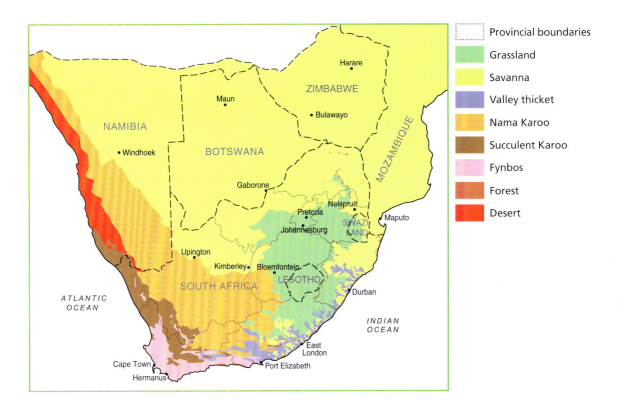

cannot survive. By the same token, the winter-rainfall region of the southwestern Cape is not suitable for plants typical of the bushveld (although Kirstenbosch Botanical Garden has performed small miracles in this regard!). In any event, although you might have some success in growing plants from other biomes and climates, they will not support the full variety of invertebrates that perform pollination services and provide a food source for birds. This is not to say that you should not grow a tree for ornamental purposes, but rather that the bulk of your garden plants should be native to the soils and climate right around you.

THE CLIMATE AND BIOMES OF SOUTHERN AFRICA

Owing to the diversity of our landscape and climate, southern Africa has a rich diversity of birds – over 900 species including residents, migrants and nomads. From the subtropical woodlands of Zimbabwe to the snowy peaks of the Drakensberg and from the semi-arid scrubland of the Kalahari to the windy crags of the Cape Peninsula, there is an astonishing range of plants, invertebrates and 'higher' animals, not to mention uncountable numbers of microscopic organisms in our soil and water.

The southern African landscape can be compared to an inverted bowl, sloping to one side, with a high central plateau falling away to a coastal plain of variable width. The Drakensberg escarpment in the east tilts upwards to an altitude of 3,400m, while the western escarpment is a more modest 900m above sea level. With the exception of the Zambezi, Okavango and Kunene (which arise in Zambia and Angola), all of the region's important rivers originate in the grasslands of the high-rainfall eastern escarpment, with the Orange–Vaal system draining west into the Atlantic, and the Limpopo, Lepelle (Olifants), Crocodile, Komati, Tugela and others flowing east into the Indian Ocean. In the southern Cape, a series of 'fold mountains' – from the

Cederberg to the Outeniqua – create a dramatically rippled landscape dominated by fynbos. Other important topographical features of the region are the tilted quartzite-based mountain ranges of the Magaliesberg, Waterberg and Soutpansberg in the northern bushveld, the eroded koppies and 'tafels' of the Karoo, and the vast Kalahari Basin filled with deep deposits of sand.

Southern Africa is divided into various vegetation zones (also known as *biomes* or *ecozones*) influenced by climate and elevation above sea level. Although our farms, cities, towns and suburbs have transformed large parts of these natural landscapes, their overall characteristics prevail.

Grassland

The temperate grassland biome occurs on the highveld and eastern escarpment and includes southern Gauteng, western Mpumalanga, most of the Free State and the slopes and foothills of the KwaZulu-Natal Drakensberg. Grasses are the dominant plants, but bulbs and herbs are also common. Owing to frost, trees and woody shrubs are confined to seasonal watercourses, koppies and sheltered kloofs. Grassland is the least protected biome – coal mining and the cultivation of maize, sunflowers and timber have consumed about 80 per cent of it. This is a summer-rainfall region, and all of the country's major rivers originate here. The city of Johannesburg lies at the heart of this biome, but many of its urban spaces are now so wooded that in parts it resembles a temperate forest.

Savanna

Extending over most of Namibia, Botswana, Zimbabwe and the northeastern parts of South Africa, vegetation here is a combination of grasses and trees. Rainfall occurs only in summer. Thorn trees such as the Knobthorn often dominate. Other distinctive species include Marula, Leadwood, Mopane and Baobab. Most of the larger protected areas fall into this biome, including Kruger, Kgalagadi, Hluhluwe-iMfolozi, Pilanesberg and Madikwe.

Valley thicket

Valley thicket consists of spiny evergreen shrubs, succulent aloes and small trees. The grass cover is sparse. This fragmented biome falls mostly in

As garden and street trees in the northern suburbs of Johannesburg have matured, the area has come to resemble a woodland or forest.
(Graeme Butchart)

the Eastern Cape and parts of KwaZulu-Natal, and receives moderate rainfall throughout the year. *Euphorbia*, *Euclea* and *Portulacaria* are among the characteristic shrub genera.

Nama Karoo
Covering most of the Northern Cape and the eastern parts of the Western Cape, this is a semi-arid biome. The landscape is characterised by flat plains interrupted by low hills and koppies. The vegetation is a mix of hardy shrubs, grasses, succulents, bulbs and annual forbs, with small trees occurring along seasonal watercourses and in sheltered kloofs. The rainfall is low and sporadic, falling mostly during the summer months.

Succulent Karoo
This is an arid biome in the central and western interior, characterised by low succulent shrubs and annual grasses. Rainfall is very scarce, occurring only in winter. Namaqualand, which is renowned for its spectacular spring-flowering daisies and lilies, falls into this biome.

Fynbos
Fynbos is characterised by fine-leaved heath-like bushes growing on sandy low-nutrient soils in the winter-rainfall region of the southwestern Cape. Species of *Erica* and *Protea* dominate, alongside annual bulbs and reed-like restios. It is one of only six botanical kingdoms on the planet and boasts more than 7,000 plant species, most of which are found nowhere else on Earth.

Forest
The region's forests are small and fragmented, occurring patchily from the slopes of Table Mountain to the Cederberg, through Tsitsikamma and the Wild Coast, to northern KwaZulu-Natal and the escarpment of Mpumalanga and Zimbabwe. Trees such as Yellowwood, White Stinkwood, Forest Bushwillow and Hard Pear are among the characteristic species. Ferns and mosses grow on the forest floor, which has a covering of leaf litter. There are several types of forest including montane (cloud) forest, coastal dune forest, dry sandforest and mangrove forest, as well as riverine forest, which occurs in ribbons along watercourses in the savanna and grassland. Plantations of pines and gums are often referred to as 'forests', but in reality these are sterile monocultures that support few organisms apart from a handful of adaptable 'generalists'.

Desert
True desert, largely devoid of trees, occurs in western Namibia. Despite the low rainfall, numerous desert-adapted plants and animals occur.

Fynbos gardens are likely to attract nectar-feeding sunbirds and sugarbirds, among many other species. Hermanus, Western Cape

Gardens in coastal strandveld are surprisingly rich in birds. Vermont, Western Cape

Leaf litter and decomposing branches provide niches for invertebrates that, in turn, attract thrushes, woodpeckers and a variety of other birds. Turaco Wood, Nelspruit

THE GARDEN

Different bird species feed in different ways and have a variety of requirements for breeding, so the most important part of establishing a bird-friendly garden is to create a diverse garden structure, offering a range of habitats and food sources.

CREATING GARDEN HABITATS

Particular animals are adapted for life within a specific type of vegetation, be it a forest, grassland or gravel plain dotted with small succulents. Birds such as Spotted Thick-knees do very well in parks, because these urban landscapes have a similar structure to the open plains that they normally inhabit. It follows that the more varied your garden's structure and vegetation, the wider the variety of birds you will attract. Essentially, this means providing a combination of plants, from ground covers to taller trees, and a mix of dense and open areas, along with hard landscaping features such as embankments or rockeries. Plants take time to mature, so it's essential to have a picture of the envisioned structure and to plan carefully.

On the pages that follow there are some ideas for creating a range of habitats that will appeal to birds and other wildlife. Within these habitats, you can also create 'microhabitats' attractive to birds and the smaller creatures on which they feed. For birds, two of the most important microhabitats are dead branches and leaf litter. These are the very things that a tidy gardener quickly removes, but the microorganisms and insects at work in the decomposing wood and rotting foliage form the base of the natural food web. Although a variety of artificial structures like feeding tables and nesting boxes can also be provided and are discussed more fully later, a natural composition of plants and habitats that provide food and nesting sites is always preferable.

Sometimes, just erecting a post in an otherwise open garden will attract certain birds. The Fiscal Flycatcher and many others sing and hunt from such perches.

Fever Trees make for an ideal gallery in larger gardens or estates. Uplands College, Mpumalanga

A shady thicket is best created around established trees. Kilmorna Manor, Mpumalanga

Carissa macrocarpa forms a neat, almost impenetrable hedge.

Tree grove

A grove is a small 'wood' or group of tall trees forming a canopy that casts shade for most or all of the day, at least in summer. It is generally situated on the edge of a property. To replicate a natural forest, there should be an understorey of shade-loving ferns or low shrubs, and leaf litter should be allowed to accumulate. Fallen branches will enable fungi, microorganisms and invertebrates to flourish. Such a habitat will appeal to the African Paradise Flycatcher as well as warblers, woodpeckers and thrushes. If you allow the grove to be as 'wild' as possible then it can form part of an undisturbed 'exclusion zone', providing a retreat for wildlife in an otherwise neat garden.

Tree Gallery

This feature consists of a number of tall trees standing together in an area of lawn. Even if the understorey of mowed grass is relatively sterile, the leafy canopy will still attract beetles and caterpillars, so birds such as cuckoos, warblers and orioles will find it appealing.

Thicket

A thicket is a dense clump of large shrubs and small trees. It can comprise several specimens of a single species, or be a mixture of various plants. From a bird's perspective, the important thing is that a thicket is fairly inaccessible and thus provides a retreat when people are active. Boubous, white-eyes and apalises are among the birds that will forage and nest here.

Hedge

Although structurally similar to a thicket, a hedge is clipped into a neat shape and typically consists of a single species. Robin-chats, coucals and mousebirds may nest in hedges. Local plants that make good hedges include *Searsia*, *Euclea*, *Dodonea* and *Carissa* species. Hedge plants that produce berries are highly attractive to bulbuls, mousebirds and other frugivores.

Shrubbery

A shrubbery is a formal or semi-formal arrangement of small shrubs and various flowering plants, typically bordering a lawn or driveway. Plants are normally chosen for their ornamental value and their blooms can attract butterflies, beetles and other pollinators that appeal to insectivorous birds.

Flowerbed

This is a bed in which small flowering plants grow in full sun, with different species on display over the seasons. Flowerbeds may be formal or semi-formal, with weeds being removed regularly. Butterflies and other pollinators will attract insectivorous birds, while plants with tubular flowers attract sunbirds and other nectar feeders.

Meadow

A more natural version of a flowerbed, a garden meadow is covered with lilies, daisies and other annuals that are left more or less to their own devices. Except for potentially suffocating blackjacks and the like, most soft-stemmed weeds are left alone to grow alongside the flowers. Birds such as canaries, waxbills and mannikins will be attracted to this habitat.

Rockery

This is a collection of boulders and rocks arranged in such a way that aloes and other succulent plants can flourish. Small *Commiphora* or *Kirkia* trees can provide light shade, but most succulent plants require full sun and need to be facing north. If your garden already contains a natural rocky outcrop, then a selection of these plants can be cultivated on the north-facing side. Skinks, agamas, thread snakes, centipedes, spiders and other wildlife will thrive in a rockery, especially if people rarely go there. Sunbirds will feed from nectar-producing plants, while flowering euphorbias lure flies and wasps, which, in turn, attract drongos and flycatchers.

Plectranthus grows rapidly and puts on a spectacular flowering show in autumn, but does require water and partial shade.

Instead of a thirsty lawn, a mixture of annual daisies, bulbs and native grasses can create an attractive meadow.

Most aloes and other succulent plants do best in a rockery where water drains away rapidly.

Lawns require watering and mowing but they are a classic feature that not only show off trees and shrubberies to best effect, but are themselves a microhabitat for birds.

ECOLOGICAL NICHES

Each species has a *niche* or role in the complex web of life (ecosystem) it inhabits. This niche is determined by how it finds food and shelter, survives and reproduces. In human terms, a niche can be compared to a profession: among birds, there are hunters, seed dispersers and pollinators. In very few cases are these ecological roles clear cut, however, since there are many overlaps, and feeding patterns often change with the seasons.

For the ecologically-minded gardener, the idea is to create habitats and microhabitats in which a variety of species, not just birds, can make a living. Having a completely manicured and 'tidy' garden might look good to many people, but very often the 'messy' parts – leaf litter, rotting branches and tangled thickets – provide more niches. And since insects and other invertebrates form an essential component in the diets of many birds, these creatures must be allowed to flourish.

Lawn

Most people love neatly clipped lawns, as they are ideal places for children and dogs to play – and many birds enjoy them too. However, keeping a lawn green and vigorous is a challenge throughout southern Africa, where we have extended dry seasons and grass rapidly dries out if it isn't watered. Kikuyu *Pennisetum clandestinum* has long been the preferred grass for lawns, including sports fields; native to the Highlands of East Africa, this creeping grass grows vigorously and can look very attractive. It may escape into natural areas, where it quickly becomes an invasive weed, especially along

Cape Wagtails find much to eat on open lawns.

watercourses. Because South Africa is a water-deficient country, more and more people are turning away from expansive lawns and looking at options such as less thirsty ground covers. However, if you still want a lawn, a number of indigenous grasses make good waterwise alternatives to kikuyu, including L.M. Grass *Dactyloctenium australe*, Kweek Grass *Cynodon dactylon* and Buffalo Grass *Stenotaphrum secundatum*. If these are allowed to flower and seed in late summer, then canaries and mannikins may arrive to harvest the crop.

Grass patch

A grass patch differs from a lawn in that the grass is not mowed or cut, but instead allowed to flower and set seed. A wide variety of grasses can be considered for this purpose, including Broad-leaved Bristle Grass *Setaria megaphylla*, Guinea Grass *Panicum maximum* and the attractive Natal Redtop *Melinis repens*. Most good indigenous nurseries sell these and other grasses and can provide advice on cultivation. Waxbills, mannikins and canaries will be attracted to this habitat.

Marsh

To create a marsh in the garden you need a wetland vegetated with sedges, bulrushes, reeds and other bog-loving plants such as *Wachendorfia* and *Kniphofia*. Best in full sun and adjacent to a pond, the marsh should be treated as an exclusion zone and left undisturbed as much as possible. Frogs, dragonflies and damselflies may take up residence and, if the marsh is sufficiently large, with tall enough vegetation, weavers and bishops may breed there.

Embankment or retaining wall

On properties with a steep gradient, embankments can be created to form one or more terraces. If a wall is preferred, then any small gaps that are left will become potential breeding sites for hoopoes and kingfishers, among others. The same result can be achieved with a more natural earthen bank, but rainfall run-off must be managed to ensure that erosion does not occur.

Grasses are most attractive to birds when they set seed in autumn.

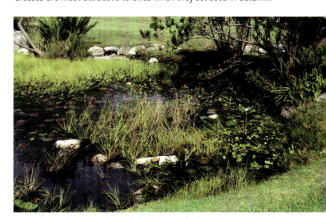
A marsh can be created simply by lining a shallow excavation with thick plastic sheeting.

Artificial embankments should be smooth to limit access by potential predators.

FIG TREE
An ecosystem in one tree

Wild figs in the genus *Ficus* make wonderful garden features, and a mature tree is host to an entire complex ecosystem of its own. Wild figs have a unique reproductive system: minuscule fig wasps pollinate the flowers within the fig. Only when these tiny hidden flowers are fertilised does the fig ripen, at which point hordes of bulbuls, barbets, white-eyes, starlings and others arrive to feast on its juicy flesh. The story does not end here, because apalises, flycatchers and swallows feed on the fig wasps, while robin-chats, hoopoes and thrushes take the beetles and bugs that live among the ripe figs that fall to the ground. Most parts of southern Africa have one or more species of native fig tree, so select one from your own area to be sure that the matching fig wasp pollination process can occur. Bear in mind that over time fig trees may become very large, so a good-sized garden is required.

Sycamore Figs *Ficus sycomorus* are suitable only for large gardens.

Cape White-eye feeding on a Strangler Fig *Ficus natalensis*

Cultivating a fig tree species native to your area will allow you to witness the fascinating cycle of life of these remarkable trees. Tiny fig wasps enter the unripe figs to pollinate the hidden flowers and start the fruiting process.

African Green Pigeons often spend hours feeding and resting within fig trees.

The Broom Cluster Fig *Ficus sur* occurs naturally over much of southern Africa. It makes an ideal garden subject because it does not grow too large.

The evident enthusiasm of birds drinking and bathing is a pleasure to watch. Cape Robin-chat, Vermont, Western Cape.

PROVIDING WATER

Not all birds need to drink, as some species get the moisture they need from their food, but others, such as seedeaters, need to drink daily. In addition, most birds like to bathe to maintain their plumage or to cool off in hot weather. With this in mind, providing water in your garden is one of the best ways to attract birds, and the drier your climate, the more appealing water will be.

Birdbaths

The simplest and most effective way to provide water for birds is with a birdbath. This can be anything from a nursery-bought pedestal to an old upturned dustbin lid, but the most important thing is where you situate it. All birds are naturally wary of people and predators such as cats and hawks. They need good visibility when drinking or bathing and are happiest when a drinking spot is away from paths, driveways, walls and windows – a minimum distance of about 3m from any of these features is advisable. Shyer birds like to be able to retreat quickly into the cover of vegetation, so it is best to position the birdbath a metre or two below an arching tree branch, or near a shrubbery. In general, it is a good idea to raise the birdbath about 1m above the ground, as this allows for a faster escape from an ambushing predator.

To encourage birds to use your drinking and bathing facility, keep the water fresh and topped up. The bath should be cleaned and scrubbed out every so often, as algae will start to grow, especially if the bath is in full sun. Consider the vantage point from which you hope to observe the avian activity – a view from the kitchen window is often preferred, but you might like to keep one eye on the birdbath while watching late afternoon TV.

Because birdbaths can become popular, it is a good idea to have more than one of them. If possible, place one in a more open area and the other in a more secluded spot, to appeal to the preferences of different species. In some regions, large numbers of doves may aggregate at drinking points, preventing waxbills or canaries

Karoo Thrush, Fourways, Gauteng

Purple-crested Turaco, Nelspruit, Mpumalanga

Common Waxbill, Vermont, Western Cape

A well-planned garden pond can be a standout feature in any garden. This large pond is at the Harold Porter Botanical Garden, Betty's Bay.

from quenching their thirst – another reason for having more than one birdbath. Do not hesitate to experiment by moving your birdbath around until you find the perfect spot.

In nature, predators often ambush prey at drinking places, and garden birdbaths are no exception. If you attract lots of doves and other thirsty birds, then do not be surprised if a goshawk or sparrowhawk takes advantage of the opportunity you have created. Witnessing a raptor or snake killing a bird in your own garden can be traumatic for the human observer, but it provides evidence of a flourishing food web.

Creating a water feature that allows water to drip or bubble into and out of a birdbath through a circulating pipe powered by a small pump can be an absolute magnet for birds. A less expensive way to make your birdbath more appealing is simply to set up a garden sprinkler next to it, so that some of the spray falls onto the water. On warm afternoons, such a set-up will attract many birds, which enjoy a thorough soaking by fanning out their wing and tail feathers under the spray. Keeping the tap at low pressure allows you to maintain the spray for a decent period without using too much water.

Ponds

Creating a natural-looking pond is among the most exciting and rewarding of garden projects, particularly for those who want to attract the widest variety of wildlife. There are many ways of going about this, depending on your budget, but the most important factor is choosing the best position for the pond. Ideally, it should be situated where it will receive good sunlight. It *is* possible to build a pond close to larger trees, but these should be on the south side of the waterbody and be sparsely foliaged, because shady pools do not attract a wide spectrum of aquatic invertebrates and do not allow you to grow flowering water lilies. A thicket or dense shrubbery on one side of the pond will suit coucals and other shy, skulking birds.

Before you start, be aware that the idea is to establish a viable aquatic ecosystem with a functioning food web of producers (algae), primary consumers (such as tadpoles and tilapia) and secondary consumers (such as predatory dragonfly larvae and, hopefully, kingfishers). If you are unsuccessful in creating this food web – and patience will be required – then you might come to regret having a pit of stagnant green water in the middle of your garden!

It is preferable, but not essential, to aerate the pond, but if you are circulating the water then you can add a small stream leading into the pond from a filtration box. If you have a large budget and plenty of space, you might consider creating a flowing system of streams, waterfalls and interlinked ponds. The tinkling sound of flowing water is certainly appealing to the human ear, and thrushes and other birds love to bathe in running water.

The most popular and economical way to create a garden pond is simply to excavate an area and then line it with strong black polythene (500 microns thick). This allows you to create a natural-looking pond wetland that has both deep areas and shallows that overflow into a marsh, where bulrushes and other bog-loving plants can grow. Ponds can also be raised above ground level in the formal style or excavated and lined with bricks and concrete. In addition, precast fibreglass garden ponds are available from some garden centres.

Water lilies and other aquatic species can remain within their pots or baskets, while fallen leaves and other plant matter can be allowed to decompose naturally in the pond, releasing oxygen and providing sustenance for snails and other aquatic herbivores. Frogs will find their own way to your pond, but fish need to be introduced. Ideally, the fish should not be fed artificially but left to their own devices to feed on algae, water organisms and insects. Common Goldfish are hardy and adaptable, but Banded Tilapia and Mozambique Tilapia are southern African natives that also do well. Care must be taken that invasive alien plants such as Water Hyacinth *Eichhornia crassipes* and Water Lettuce *Pistia stratiotes* do not get into your pond or wetland, as these grow vegetatively and can

Ponds should ideally have a shallow fringe, to prevent non-aquatic wildlife from drowning.

Birds, frogs and fish may not be the only ones keen to access a garden pond!

By circulating water, you can create a small stream that both oxygenates the pond and provides a relaxing sound.

The Cape River Frog gives a series of croaking calls that add atmosphere to the garden pond.

Dragonflies, such as this Broad Scarlet, may visit or take up residence at a garden pond.

Hamerkops may visit garden ponds to prey on toads and frogs.

For bird gardeners, a visit from a dazzling Malachite Kingfisher is arguably the highlight of any garden pond project.

be transported to rivers and wild wetlands on the legs of egrets or herons, where they can choke up waterways. Some careless nurseries still sell these invasive aquatic plants as ornamentals, not realising that it is irresponsible and illegal to do so.

A garden pond is likely to attract toads (Guttural, Raucous or Red toads, depending on your region) and large numbers of these amphibians may congregate to breed in spring and early summer. Male toads advertise to females with very loud calls ('Guttural' and 'Raucous' are appropriate names), a seasonal nocturnal cacophony that your neighbours may not especially appreciate, even if you do! However, the numerous tadpoles produced by the toads play a vital role in consuming algae and mosquito larvae, and dragonfly larvae, carnivorous fishes and kingfishers prey on them in turn.

Swimming pools

In hot weather, some birds will splash-bathe in swimming pools to cool down. The African Paradise Flycatcher and Brown-hooded Kingfisher are two such dippers. Swallows and swifts will skim the swimming pool surface to drink, and nightjars may do the same after dark. Because moths, beetles and other insects frequently drown in swimming pools, flycatchers and wagtails will swoop down and snatch them up. Swimming pools are often a death trap for shrews, rodents, toads, snakes and other creatures, but you can reduce these unnatural wildlife mortalities by leaving a small plank floating in the water and checking it each morning.

Perhaps the ultimate water feature is a natural swimming pool with a biological filtration system. Bacteria and microbes living within the roots of bulrushes and other aquatic plants purify the water, so chemicals are not required. This can be expensive to create and maintain, but is a fulfilling project for the truly committed environmental gardener.

Oudebosch Eco-Cabins swimming pool with bulrush filter at Kogelberg Biosphere Reserve, Western Cape

FEATHER CARE AND DUST BATHING

Feathers are crucial for flight and regulating body temperature. Although all birds moult once a year, individual feathers wear down over time, and considerable effort goes into caring for them. Preening is the process whereby a bird straightens and smoothes its feathers by combing and stroking them, using its bill to 'zip up' or straighten out the barbules. Bathing is another important means of maintaining feather condition, and birds tackle this in different ways. Robin-chats and white-eyes are among the birds that enjoy bathing in water, but others such as mousebirds, bee-eaters and sparrows prefer to dust bathe, letting the fine dust particles absorb sticky plant resins or juices. Another aspect of feather care is the removal of external parasites, which is accomplished by basking in the sun with feathers raised to expose the bare skin. A patch of fine bare soil in a quiet spot will provide dust-bathing opportunities in your garden.

Speckled Mousebirds are habitual dust bathers.

Four species come to a feeding station at The Retreat at Groenfonetin, Klein Karoo: Cape Weaver, Speckled Mousebird, Cape Sparrow and House Sparrow.

PROVIDING FOOD

There are two approaches to feeding birds in your garden. The first, and easiest, is to place supplementary foods where birds can find them. The second, more sustainable, tactic is to grow plants that provide edible berries and seeds or plants that attract the invertebrates that birds like to eat. A combination of these two methods works best.

In northern Europe and North America the typically harsh winters prompt millions of people to feed garden birds, which has spurred on the growth of a multimillion-dollar industry. Gardening outlets stock a wide variety of packaged seeds, peanuts, suet treats and fat balls, as well as various feeders in which these foods can be placed. These products are attractively branded and cleverly marketed, and bird conservation agencies such as Audubon and the Royal Society for the Protection of Birds (RSPB) generate major revenues from their sale. In the UK, it is estimated that half the population feeds birds in the garden, so the amount of money involved is not hard to imagine. A smaller percentage of Americans actually feed birds, but with a larger human population, the bird-feeding business is enormous.

Unsurprisingly, there has been debate over the issue of artificially feeding birds. Does it create a dependence on humans? Does it allow some species to proliferate unnaturally? Does it reduce natural mortality or impair the immune system? Can contaminated foods spread disease?

To a greater or lesser extent, all of these are valid issues, but given that the natural habitat has been so greatly modified by urban development, the 'helping hand' might be justified. In this regard, the RSPB and Audubon go to great lengths to

The Grey Go-away-bird is an omnivore and may visit a braai grid to collect scraps.

provide educational materials and raise awareness of responsible and safe feeding strategies, stressing that supplementary food cannot provide *all* of the vital proteins that young and adult birds require, so creating and managing one's garden to provide a source of natural foods is vital.

Although the high plateau and mountains of southern Africa can get bitterly cold for short spells in winter, we do not experience the protracted weeks of snow and hard weather that are a feature of winters in the northern hemisphere. This means that rarely, if ever, are birds threatened with seasonal starvation in our region.

Most birds are opportunistic and will take the easiest option when it comes to feeding. As with the positioning of a birdbath, you need to choose a site for your bird-feeding station (or stations) where you can view the birds that visit without appearing to pose a threat. Feeding birds do not want to be disturbed, and they require good visibility so that they can keep an eye out for would-be predators. A minimum distance of about 3m from a building or pathway is therefore recommended, and the feeding platform should be 1–1.5m off the ground.

Doves, spurfowl and sparrows are among the birds that are quite happy feeding on the ground,

The Cape Sugarbird does not eat fruit, but this individual was tempted to sip on the juice of a sweet watermelon in Vermont, Western Cape.

but seed and grain scattered in this way can become messy and drain away into unwanted areas after rain. To allow small finches such as waxbills and canaries to feed without being overwhelmed by doves, it is advisable to place seed in a hanging feeder with a small lip on which doves cannot balance.

Seeds and Dry Food

Seeds are the most popular type of bird food but will, of course, only attract seedeaters. There are many different kinds of seed, which can be bought individually or in mixtures. Among others, the Thick-billed Weaver and Brimstone Canary relish sunflower seeds and peanuts, while the Bronze Mannikin and Common Waxbill enjoy the small millet or 'budgie seed'. Since few birds can consume them, avoid buying seed mixtures that contain dried beans, lentils and rice, which are often added to bulk up cheaper products. Some 'bird food' packs also contain pink or green dog biscuit chunks that have to be soaked to render them edible. On the topic of dog food, robin-chats and boubous may eat leftover food or kibble in a backyard dog bowl, but it is unclear what effect this has on a bird's digestive system in large amounts, so deliberate provisioning should be avoided.

Tearing up chunks of soft bread and placing them out for birds is not recommended as this, too,

Birds such as these White-backed Mousebirds, Sociable Weavers and Cape Sparrows are happy to feed on the ground.

You never can tell who might show up at your bird table – this young African Goshawk is feeding on bonemeal in a Hoedspruit garden.

may pose a digestive problem for birds. Rather let the stale bread dry out and then break it up into crumbs. Wholewheat bread with visible grains is usually fine. Most moulds are harmless, but some may cause respiratory infections in birds, so do not put out mouldy bread or leave uneaten fruit to become mouldy. Rice and breakfast cereal are safe to feed to birds but should be dry.

Fruit

Almost any kind of fruit will attract birds, and it is possible to choreograph quite spectacular feeding bouts. You may be able to get a regular supply of bruised or overripe fruit from your local fruit shop for free or at a reduced price. A ripe pawpaw sliced in half and placed on a feeding platform in a Gauteng garden during winter may attract 20 or more Grey Go-away-birds along with barbets, bulbuls, starlings and white-eyes – the pink flesh dripping with sweet sticky juice proving quite impossible for the birds to ignore!

Apples, bananas, peaches, pears, grapes, oranges or melons – you name it and frugivores will eat it. To prevent fruit from rolling off, your feeding platform should have a lip or stakes (nails are good enough) onto which the fruits can be spiked. Another option is simply to hammer a few nails into a thick branch, being careful not to drive them in too deep and damage the tree, and then spike fruit onto them.

An interesting sideshow can occur if some fruit remains uneaten on the feeding platform, as flies then appear and they, in turn, may attract flycatchers and drongos.

Rather than putting out the same amount of fruit every day, arrange erratic fruit banquets that pull in birds on a more random basis. In this way, they won't become dependent on your supply and will continue feeding on native berries and performing their important ecological role as seed dispersers.

Bonemeal and fat

Bonemeal is a mixture of ground animal bones and butcher's offcuts. In coarse form it can be put out on bird feeders, where it is highly attractive to many birds, including shrikes, drongos and robin-chats, and may even lure shy birds such as coucals. Since it is high in protein and phosphorus, most nurseries sell a finely ground-up version for use as an organic plant fertiliser, but this is not suitable for feeding to birds.

Many insectivorous birds will eat animal fat; cakes of lard or suet containing seeds, ground nuts and grated cheese can be very alluring.

Excess fat from cooking meat is said to be bad for birds, although the Familiar Chat is known as the *spekvreter* (='fat-eater') in Afrikaans, for its

Crested Barbet feeding on butcher's bonemeal.

habit of eating the animal fat used to grease ox-wagon wheels in days of old. If you enjoy braaiing outdoors, don't be surprised if boubous and barbets arrive to help to clean up the grid! Margarine and canola oil should never be provided for birds, as these can easily stick to feathers, destroying their insulation and waterproof properties (just as penguins are affected by an oil spill).

Live food
Some people question the use of living creatures as bait for birds, but if you are willing, it can be rewarding both for the birds and their provider. The most popular and easy-to-manage form of live food is undoubtedly the lowly mealworm. This is the larval (grub) form of the Mealworm Beetle *Tenebrio molitor*, a cosmopolitan species that is considered a pest by commercial grain farmers; colonisation and international trade have facilitated the spread of this species around the world.

Some pet shops sell live mealworms, but it is easy enough to raise them yourself. Once you obtain a few from a pet shop or mealworm farmer, release them into a large bucket filled up halfway with bran (the ground-up husks of cereal grain). Slice up a few apples or potatoes and place them on the top, then punch some holes in the lid for aeration before closing it. Fine gauze stretched over the top of the lid will prevent fruitflies and other small insects from getting in through the holes. The bran should be kept moist but not wet, and within a week you'll have a thriving colony of mealworms from which you can harvest a daily handful. Remember to keep feeding them with potato peels and the like. They should be offered in a steep-sided container from which they cannot escape too quickly. In time, certain birds may take these protein-rich crawlers from your hands.

Many are the keen mealworm farmers who have bulbuls, drongos, robin-chats and bush-shrikes eating these wriggling grubs out of their hands, although one ought to be careful of a hook-billed Bokmakierie taking more than it is offered! Dried mealworms are now available at some

Mealworms (the larvae of the Mealworm Beatle) are irresistible to many birds and can be 'farmed' at home.

outlets, but for birds they never have the appeal of the fresh, writhing grubs.

Another way to provide live food is to create and maintain a compost heap in your back garden. This will attract a variety of herbivorous beetles (including Rhinoceros Beetles) that will lay their eggs in the decomposing grass cuttings and other plant material. Once these hatch and turn into larvae, they will be sought out by thrushes and shrikes. Flies and other winged insects visiting the compost heap may attract flycatchers and swallows.

Goldfish in a pond might also be considered 'live food' if you are intent on having kingfishers or herons as garden visitors. Thick-knees, nightjars and owls will take moths, crickets, roaches and other nocturnal insects attracted to a light left on at night.

Nectar
Bees, wasps, butterflies, moths and birds are among the pollinators that are attracted to the sweet, energy-rich liquid nectar produced by the nectary glands of flowers. To reach this treat, pollinators have to brush the reproductive structures of a flower. Using nectar to lure pollinators has driven the evolution of plants, while finding ways to exploit this food source has

Beetles, bugs and caterpillars may defoliate some plants, but birds quickly take advantage of the insect supply, and trees and shrubs will recover.

Sunbirds, such as this female Malachite and male Southern Double-collared, come regularly to sugar-water feeders and can provide plenty of entertainment in small gardens. The solution need not be coloured, as long as the spout of the bottle is red, but once your local birds have sampled the liquid, there will be no stopping them. Onrus Gardens, Western Cape

simultaneously driven the evolution of pollinators: hence the curved shape of a sunbird's bill closely matches the length and structure of the flower tubes from which it feeds. The sugar content of nectar is about 50 per cent sucrose, 25 per cent fructose and 25 per cent glucose.

In the USA, Central and South America, many people attract hummingbirds with sugar-water feeders. This is done less for altruistic reasons than to lure these glittering little marvels close enough to watch. Gaudy plastic containers with spouts resembling red flowers are filled with sugar water and hung from trees or porches, and the hummingbirds soon arrive. In places such as Arizona, Costa Rica, Ecuador and Peru, hummingbird-feeding stations have been established to attract casual tourists as well as serious bird photographers, such that the birds provide an income for small businesses and the motivation to protect the natural habitats where they breed.

African sunbirds enjoy a similar diet to that of American hummingbirds – although they perch rather than hover while they feed – and the idea of attracting them into gardens with artificial feeders has caught on in southern Africa. Sugar-water feeders (bottles with red spouts) are available at garden centres, nurseries and weekend markets, although they are easy enough to make yourself. These feeders are appearing in gardens across the land, where up to four or five species of sunbird, as well as weavers and white-eyes, may be attracted to even the smallest of suburban plots. However, artificial feeders are not only somewhat unsightly, they also create the possibility of birds becoming dependent upon them. A good case might be made for using them in very built-up areas, but a variety of nectar-providing plants (*Aloe* and *Tecomaria* are a good start) is preferable in a reasonably sized garden.

At any rate, great care must be taken when making and providing a sweet sugar solution.

The artificial sweetener xylitol is a sugar alcohol popular among diabetics and slimmers. It comes both in pill form, to be dropped into tea or coffee, and in granulated form for use in baked products, lozenges, chewing gum, peanut butter and toothpaste. Considered safe for humans, xylitol is toxic to birds. In a recent incident in Hermanus, over 30 Cape Sugarbirds died after drinking a xylitol solution from a bird feeder. Xylitol is thought to trigger a dramatic insulin release, causing an irreversible drop in blood sugar. The moral of this sad story is that if you wish to attract nectivorous birds to an artificial feeder, *use only dissolved table sugar*. Four parts water to one part table sugar should be boiled and then allowed to cool before being poured into the feeding bottle. It is not necessary to add any colourant, as long as the spout of the feeder is red. Finally, it is important to change the sugar mixture daily to prevent fungal infections from spreading to the feeding birds.

PROVIDING NEST SITES

If you have a few mature trees and shrubs in your garden, then doves, bulbuls, mousebirds, white-eyes, sunbirds, sparrows, weavers and others are probably already nesting in them; these are among the species that are not especially discriminating about nest placement and are content to breed close to people.

If you view your garden as a long-term project, then it is feasible to plant particular trees and shrubs with breeding birds in mind. A Fever Tree *Vachellia xanthophloea* that exceeds 3m in height (about five years of growth) will be coveted by weavers, which will stitch their nests onto the drooping outer branches. Sweet Thorn *Vachellia karroo*, Black Monkey Thorn *Senegalia mellifera* and other shrubby thorn trees provide very attractive nest sites for waxbills, mannikins and bush-shrikes, which appreciate the heavily armed branches for deterring nest predators. Fast-growing, high-branching trees such as White Stinkwood *Celtis africana* can provide suitable

This Crested Barbet has found lodging and meals in the same place – a Fourways garden!

forks in which Hadeda Ibis or African Goshawk can build their stick nests.

Swallows and martins often build their mud-pellet nests in the corners of ceilings under porches, verandas, door overhangs or open-sided buildings. Sadly, many people who find these species breeding around their houses break down the nests (sometimes repeatedly), because the birds' droppings are considered 'too messy'. For those who appreciate having swallows and martins around, it is possible to create a structure specifically for these birds.

33

Nest of a White-browed Robin-chat at the base of an old tree stump, Nelspruit

NEST BOXES FOR SUBURBAN OWLS

Having a pair of owls nesting on your property is a dream come true for anyone interested in birds and keen to create a natural garden. Not only do they control rats and other rodents, owls are also among the most captivating and fascinating of birds. In recent years, more and more people have taken to erecting nest boxes for owls, and these are now easily obtainable at garden centres, nurseries and online; they are also fairly easy to build yourself.

The two most common suburban owls in southern Africa are the Spotted Eagle- and Western Barn owls, but bear in mind that pairs of these birds typically space themselves between 500m and 2km apart. (Although in a rodent outbreak, Western Barn Owls may nest as close as 50m to one another!). Remember that if owls are already living in your suburb, they are likely to have existing breeding sites, so it may take time for them to occupy even a perfectly situated nest box, if they choose it at all.

Old gnarled trees – especially willows and oaks – have natural rot-holes where branches have fallen off, and these sites appeal to birds like hoopoes, barbets, flycatchers, tits, starlings and owls. You can create similar breeding niches by securing vessels such as old tins, kettles, pipes and the like in out-of-sight recesses or on walls.

Nesting boxes can be bought or built out of plywood in dimensions appropriate for the species you hope to attract. Smaller birds such as starlings, wrynecks, kingfishers, rollers and owlets prefer a snug nest cavity: the entrance hole should never be too large, as this makes it accessible to predators, and the birds will reject it. Bigger owls, such as the Spotted Eagle-Owl and African Wood Owl, prefer a cavity with a large entrance or one side that is fully open (see box).

Putting up nesting logs for barbets and woodpeckers and watching them inspect and then breed in them is immensely rewarding. These birds excavate their own nests, but may later be pushed out by starlings or kingfishers that breed in holes but are unable to make their own. Garden centres and nurseries sell sisal logs, and these seem to be the most successful substrate, but rough willow or poplar logs of at least 1m are also attractive to barbets. The soft wood of these invasive alien trees is ideal, and you can even encourage the process by carving out the beginnings of a hole.

Most importantly, logs and nest boxes need to be in an appropriate position, taking aspect and height

It is important that owl boxes are cleaned out at least once a year.

Left: Owl boxes can be placed in trees or on walls, but should always be in the most sheltered position possible.
Above: Observing an owl pair raise their offspring is both educational and entertaining.

Eagle-owls need an open-sided box, while barn owls require one with a small entrance. Bees may find the box before an owl pair does and, although we should all be encouraging these industrious pollinators, an active hive in the garden can be dangerous for children and pets, and will obviously deter owls. One option that has proven effective is to line the inside apex of the roof with slippery plastic sheeting to which the bees cannot affix their comb. It is important to line the base of the owl box with fine ('pea') gravel, about an inch thick, and to clean out the box (whether used by owls or not) at least once a year.

The Spotted Eagle-Owl can become extremely tame and the pairs breeding at Kirstenbosch in Cape Town and Delta Park in Johannesburg have been watched and photographed by hundreds if not thousands of people over the years. However, some eagle-owls can be very defensive and will attack people and dogs if they feel their young are threatened.

The African Wood Owl likes to breed in natural tree cavities at a height of between 1 and 2m, so anyone living in the wooded suburbs of Durban, Port Elizabeth and Nelspruit, or in the Constantia-Newlands area of Cape Town, might try positioning an owl box at an appropriate position for these birds.

Owls that are born and raised in a particular type of nest site typically look for the same setting when they are mature enough to breed themselves. Because of this, suburban owl-box owls spawn more owl-box owls!

In Johannesburg and Cape Town, hundreds of homeowners have joined the EcoSolutions Owl Box Project (**http://ecosolutions.co.za/owl-box-project**) and, although one has to pay for the box and installation as well as an annual on-site service (optional), the funds go towards the organisation's highly successful Township Owl Project, which runs owl-education programmes at schools and erects owl boxes in impoverished areas where rodents are plentiful. Orphan owls are also released in the townships, and these events attract much interest and participation from children, teachers and parents.

above ground into account. They should be at least 2m above the ground and face away from prevailing rain and wind. Logs can be placed at a slight angle, so that the excavated hole does not receive direct sunlight and overheat. The birds themselves will tell you whether you have made the right choice. It is often a process of trial and error; so don't think twice about moving the nest box after a while if birds show no interest in it. Bear in mind that the majority of birds begin their breeding cycles in August or September, so a nest box put up in March will most certainly be ignored, even if it is in a desirable place. At the right time of year, however, barbets have been known to inspect and begin excavating a sisal log within an hour of its being erected!

With the advent of remote cameras, an exciting opportunity exists to observe and digitally record activity around and even inside the nest chamber without disturbing the occupants. Nest-cams, designed specifically for placement *inside* nesting boxes, are now very popular in Britain. 'Trail' or 'wildlife' cameras are digital cameras that can shoot still images or video. Being weatherproof, they are intended to be mounted *outside*, hidden from view if necessary, where they can capture still images at specific intervals or record video when they detect motion. The cameras can be left in the same place for months, and fascinating or unusual behaviour can be documented.

There is often fierce competition for perfectly placed nest boxes or logs, and this can result in fights and evictions among different species. In some cases, an aggressive challenger might kill another bird or its young. It can be difficult to watch this play out in your own garden, but it is always best to let nature take its course. Interestingly, rivals of the same species generally avoid hurting each other when competing for nest sites.

Having a pair of owls breeding on your property is one of the ultimate garden bird experiences, and an interesting aspect of having owls breeding or roosting in your garden is the opportunity to collect their pellets and examine them to determine the diet of these nocturnal hunters.

DANGERS FACING GARDEN BIRDS

Many birds will move into the garden spaces we create, and over time individuals may come to trust us. This is in sharp contrast with most wild birds, which regard humans as predators and flee at our approach. Having encouraged birds into our gardens, it becomes our responsibility to ensure that they come to no undue harm. Some of the dangers that birds might face when they live alongside people are obvious, while others are less so.

The Red-chested Cuckoo feeds primarily on caterpillars, so insecticides targeting these larval butterflies and moths can have disastrous results.

Pesticides

Many people use chemical pesticides and herbicides to control weeds and unwanted creatures in their gardens, typically aphids, cutworms, snails, slugs, bugs, crickets and mole rats. War is also waged against spiders, ants and other invertebrates. Bear in mind that animals that eat roots, leaves, buds and flowers, or cause them to wilt, were either in the area before the suburbs were built or have appeared on the scene to take advantage of the new flora.

If your main objective in the garden is to attract birds, then you should leave the pest control to them and do your best to tolerate *all* wildlife. It may take time for particular birds to arrive and prey upon aggregations of invertebrates that are damaging plants, but it is better to give up on the affected plants than use chemicals that will have ripple effects down the food chain and may even harm your own pets and children. The problem with using pesticides, herbicides and rodenticides is that their broader impact is not usually seen until it is too late.

Even if you never use pesticides in your own garden, you may find that your neighbours do so, and this will obviously impact on the birds and other wildlife that you are trying to encourage. A bit of knowledge about pesticides may be useful in conversations with people around you.

Snails are probably at the top of the gardener's hate list, as these gastropods use their coarse mouthparts to munch through new plant growth, including flower buds. The most common snail throughout most of South Africa is the alien European Brown Snail *Cornu aspersum*, but the White Garden Snail *Theba pisana* is another invasive species that can form unnaturally large and damaging populations in gardens in the southern Cape. There are, of course, indigenous snails. In reasonable numbers, they play an important role in breaking down humus, so are viewed as desirable by the ecologically-minded gardener. Commercial 'snail bait' products are made from a highly toxic compound called metaldehyde, flavoured with molasses, apple and bran to attract snails. Unfortunately, dogs find this a tasty treat and can become very ill or even die of secondary poisoning. Thrushes and other birds that might eat the dead or dying snails will be similarly affected. Snail bait is also available in liquid and powder form, which can get onto paws and be licked off when cats or dogs groom themselves. Furthermore, many of these products also contain insecticides that make them even more toxic. Iron phosphate is a 'molluscicide' used for killing slugs and snails and, although safer for dogs and cats than metaldehyde, its effects on the entire food chain are largely unknown.

Salt is said to repel snails, but the best way to reduce the population of snails in your garden is to collect them at night when they are active. Simply walk around with a torch and pluck them off the vegetation. Depending on your sensibilities (or those of your children) you can crush them and add them to your compost heap or remove them to a distant spot.

In some parts of the country, people who spend a lot of time manicuring their lawns get rather upset when random mounds of soil keep appearing overnight. These are the workings of mole rats – sizeable vegetarian rodents, not to be confused with the much smaller and insectivorous golden moles, which leave only raised furrows as they move about underground. Since mole rats spend most of their time underground, they are virtually impossible to catch, so poison bait is often thrown down their entry holes. If the rodent dies underground, beetles will consume it and probably die too. If the mole rat comes to the surface in distress, it is likely to be seized by a cat or an owl, which may then die of secondary poisoning. Ecologically-minded gardeners simply have to accept the mole rats and let them carry on with their lives.

Predation by pets

Studies in the UK have estimated that domestic cats catch and kill about 55 million birds every year. However, the birds caught most frequently are common generalist species that have adapted to human-altered landscapes, and there is no evidence that predation by cats is having any impact on

Domestic cats take large numbers of garden birds, but mostly the commonest species.

bird populations. Cats are also thought to target inexperienced juveniles, weaker and older birds, which are 'expendable' in terms of population dynamics. In Australia, New Zealand and on smaller islands where cats have been introduced, it is quite different, since birds in these places did not evolve alongside any native cat-like predators and thus lack the necessary evasive instincts. In these countries there is a far greater need to control cats, as they have a significant impact on bird populations.

Here in South Africa humans have, to a large extent, removed or displaced the majority of native predators from urban areas. Where once a genet or jackal might have preyed upon a dove or sparrow, it's the domestic cat that kills it now, and doves anyway occur in abnormally high densities when seed food is provisioned all around the neighbourhood. Nevertheless, a Siamese bringing in a dead flufftail or twinspot to the bird-loving gardener will not be viewed sympathetically, and some owners opt for fitting their cat's collar with a small bell, although this can be risky for the cat. Many dogs, especially those that belong to the terrier group, have predatory instincts and may attack and catch birds, although they generally lack the cunning and patience of cats.

Nest predation by monkeys

African birds have evolved alongside monkeys and have breeding strategies that allow them to withstand predation of their eggs and nestlings by these arboreal primates. However, in parts of KwaZulu-Natal, Limpopo and Mpumalanga, Vervet Monkeys may become regular garden visitors, being attracted to the food that is provided for birds, and taking up residence in some neighbourhoods. While waiting for easy feeding opportunities, these intelligent primates may conduct meticulous searches for nests, as they relish the prospect of adding bird eggs and nestlings to their diet. This can lead to unnaturally high nest failure and can become a major challenge. Feeding birds should be discontinued if you want the monkeys to forage elsewhere, at least during the peak bird breeding season, from August to November.

The African Pygmy Kingfisher flies low and fast, and is a frequent victim of window strikes; some individuals, such as this Hoedspruit bird, are only stunned and soon recover.

Collisions with windows

A common cause of mortality among garden birds is colliding with glass windows. Certain species are more prone to this than others, with fast-flying doves being top of the list. Young, inexperienced goshawks and sparrowhawks may also come to grief during high-speed chases. Brown-hooded Kingfishers often collide with windows, and in bushveld regions the tiny African Pygmy Kingfisher, which flies at great speed like a low dart, is a frequent victim. Collisions are not always fatal, and sometimes a concussed bird just needs to be placed in a warm, dark box for a while so that it can recover. However, there's little hope of escape after a window collision if dogs and cats are prowling about. The most popular way of alleviating this problem is to place decals on windows and glass doors, as these shapes create a visual disturbance in what birds otherwise perceive as an open flyway.

Territorial birds that see their reflection in windows may engage in tireless battles with imaginary rivals. It may be entertaining to watch for a while but is detrimental to the attacker, and annoying to the homeowner in the long run. The problem can usually be solved by placing some object on the windowsill inside, or by sticking decals or paper on the glass to eliminate or break up the reflection.

Caring for sick or injured birds

From time to time, we encounter a bird that appears to be in trouble. It could be one that has been attacked by a pet or flown into a window, or it may have fallen from a nest.

The first thing to establish is whether the bird is actually injured and needs help. In handling a bird, one has to be firm and decisive, because damage to wing bones can occur easily if the bird thrashes about. The best procudure is to drape a tea towel over the bird and then place it gently in a closed shoebox for half an hour. In many cases, a bird simply needs to calm down before flying off. Bear in mind that many young birds are presumed to be in trouble when they are in fact simply going through the early stages of independence. Estimating the general life stage is therefore important.

If the bird is fully feathered, with no fleshy base to its gape, then it is beyond the fledging stage and your intervention may save its life. If the bird is unwilling or unable to escape after 30 minutes in a dark box or cloth bag, then it should be taken to a vet or local wildlife rehabilitation centre for inspection; if you are not aware of a local individual or centre, then social media can be very useful in finding an appropriate person in your area.

If the bird is naked or only partially feathered, it is a nestling and has left its nest prematurely. This may have been caused by wind, sibling activity or bailing out at the approach of a predator. The latter is unlikely, as such a predator would typically take *all* the nestlings. If the nestling appears uninjured and you can find the nest, the best option is to put it back. It is a myth that nestlings touched by human hands will be ignored by their parents and starve. If the nest itself has blown down, then you can try to rebuild it or construct an artificial nest, place the nestling in that, and then wait for the parents to find and feed it. The instinct of parent birds to respond to the begging calls of their young is very strong. If the parents do not return to feed the nestling, then you can try hand feeding it yourself, or take the bird to a vet or wildlife rehabilitation centre, but its chances of survival are very low at this point.

In the case of fledgling birds, 'help' often becomes harm. The process of fledging involves jumping out of the nest, and most baby birds need at least three days to learn how to fly, as their feathers are not yet fully formed. During this period, their parents feed them in low bushes or on the ground, urging them to move from place to place, and they may scramble into thickets when danger threatens. Well-meaning people often 'rescue' these birds, but even if they survive through hand feeding (which most don't), they will usually struggle to adjust to life, as they missed out on the vital education provided by their parents.

Top: This nestling dove is being fed with a mixture of oatmeal and vegetable oil. **Above:** This Tambourine Dove has been killed by flying into a glass window.

Cape White-eye feeding on the nectar of a Dune Aloe.

THE BIRDS

Birds are a joy in the garden, but one that is all too easy to take for granted. Learning to identify birds is much less daunting if you first get to know and identify those species visiting your neighbourhood and start observing their fascinating behaviour.

WATCHING BIRDS

Watching birds is not only relaxing and pleasurable, but paying close attention to their behaviour will lead to greater understanding of their activities.

Most birders keep lists of the birds they see. This may include a list of species they've observed in a particular place, like their garden, and a 'life list' of all the species that they've ever seen anywhere. Such lists are fun to compile and give one a sense of accomplishment. Lists can also be a valuable source of information for data collectors, so it is vital that they are accurate.

Much of what we know today about bird behaviour has been derived from simple observations made by amateur bird-watchers, and some common garden birds still have secrets to reveal.

If you wish to document your observations of garden birds, then you should submit them to a bird club newsletter or to Ornithological Observations, a digital journal published by the Animal Demography Unit at the University of Cape Town (see p.186).

Joining a local bird club and getting out and about with more experienced birders, beyond the garden, is also a wonderful way to improve your bird-watching skills.

The Black-collared Barbet has a robust bill, suitable for excavating a nesting cavity in soft wood.

BIRD ANATOMY

Birds range in size from the Common Ostrich, which weighs up to 125kg, to the world's smallest bird, the Bee Hummingbird of Cuba, which is 80,000 times lighter and weighs just 1.6g. The smallest African bird is the Cape Penduline-tit, weighing in at about 7g, while waxbills and firefinches are only marginally heavier. However, no matter their size, they all have a broadly similar skeleton, with forelimbs modified into wings, and lightweight bones in order to facilitate flight.

Their bill shapes, by contrast, are extraordinarily diverse. Most birds must grasp, pluck or hold their food with the beak alone, so as you start observing the birds in your garden, these different bill shapes will give clues about various species' food preferences. For example, a long, slender bill is typically used for sipping nectar from tubular flowers, whereas a hooked bill might be used for tearing meat.

A second characteristic in which bird species differ strongly from one another is in the length and shape of their legs, feet and toes. Feet are used for perching, hopping, walking, running, preening, paddling and for grasping prey, and they too can provide you with clues when watching and identifying avian visitors.

Birds have different types of feathers, arranged in particular zones such as the mantle, nape and vent. It's important to become familiar with the terminology used for feathers, as they provide most of the external identifying features of a bird and are constantly used in bird identification guides. (See the diagram below, which shows the different feather groups and body parts.)

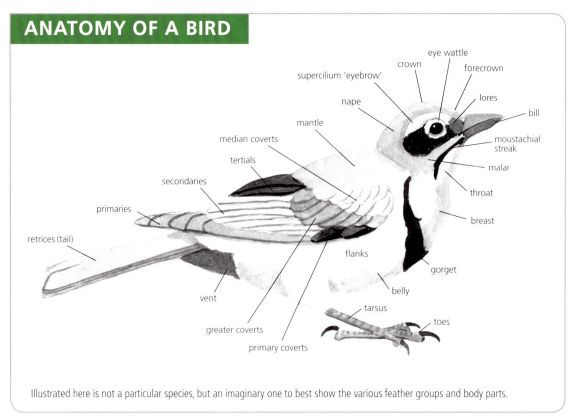

ANATOMY OF A BIRD

Illustrated here is not a particular species, but an imaginary one to best show the various feather groups and body parts.

BIRD NAMES

For many people, beginners and advanced students alike, bird names may be a source of confusion and debate, sometimes even acrimony! Under the classification system, each bird (like other living things) is given a double-barrelled name. These names are written in italics: the first part is the bird's genus name, which always has a capital letter, e.g. *Cossypha*; the second part is its species name, which is lower case, e.g. *caffra*. The genus indicates that bird's relationships within the scientific classification hierarchy, while the species refers to its specific characteristics.

Birds also have one or more vernacular (common) names. Although the scientific names of birds are often fascinating and revealing in their own right, few people bother with them, preferring instead to identify birds by their common names. Some common names are descriptive and refer to noteworthy traits (e.g. Fork-tailed Drongo); others refer to regions (e.g. Karoo Prinia); in some cases a bird is named in someone's honour or after the person who discovered it (e.g. Burchell's Coucal). In 2005, many common English bird names were altered or changed when the 7th edition of *Roberts Birds of Southern Africa* was published. These changes were made for good reason – to standardise bird names across Africa and the world – but nevertheless confused and even annoyed many people, some of whom still prefer to use the former names.

BIRD CALLS

Birds call for a range of reasons, from laying claim to a territory, to attracting mates, to raising the alarm at the approach of a predator. Because calls are often the only indication that a bird is present in your garden, especially if it is shy or concealed in thick vegetation, they are an immensely valuable aid in bird identification.

When you hear calls in your garden, try to locate and then focus on the bird that's making the sound, watch it closely and pay attention to the rhythm, phrases and regularity of the call. Also bear in mind that each species will make a variety of different sounds.

There are also many excellent bird-call apps available that can help you to expand your knowledge of bird calls (see p.187), but it is important to use these responsibly: playing calls outside may alarm and disturb birds and interfere with their natural behaviour.

Getting out, beyond the garden, with more experienced birders can help you improve your bird-watching skills. Woodbush Forest, Tzaneen

FEEDING BEHAVIOUR

Various adaptations determine the way in which birds find and consume their food. Some birds are *specialised* feeders, taking mainly one type of food, while others are *generalised* feeders that take different kinds of food depending on seasonal availability or particular needs. Most of the birds that occur regularly in gardens are generalists, able to eat a variety of foods, with the exception of the specialised nectar-feeding sunbirds.

Among birds there are feeding groups such as *frugivores*, *granivores*, *nectarivores* and *carnivores*. The carnivores are further divided into groups such as insectivores and piscivores. Generalists, such as bulbuls and starlings, fall into two or more groups.

BREEDING BEHAVIOUR

All birds establish a breeding territory of some kind, in which a pair can find sufficient food, build or occupy a nest and raise their young. In order to maintain and defend these territories, birds must advertise their presence by singing and vocalising, moving repeatedly throughout their territory, or simply by perching in a conspicuous place.

Some gregarious species, such as doves, weavers and sparrows, do not have territories, apart from the immediate vicinity of their nest.

At the onset of the breeding season, most birds perform courtship rituals, either to find a mate or to cement the bond between existing partners; in some species, these displays are elaborate, even dramatic. Birds are typically most vocal at this time, and some species perform conspicuous flight displays. In South Africa, September (the 'southern spring') marks the onset of breeding for the majority of smaller birds, although, in the winter-rainfall regions of the Cape, some species breed in June.

For birds, mating is invariably a brief affair, but nest building can take several weeks depending on the species.

Once the eggs are laid, the female usually incubates them alone, but this responsibility

The Violet-backed Starling **(top)** and Cape Bulbul **(above)** are generalists that feed on insects or fruit according to availability.

is shared in the case of the African Paradise Flycatcher, the mousebirds and others. The females of many bird species have duller plumage than the males so that they blend in with their nest surroundings. Species that lay their eggs on the ground in a scrape, such as the Spotted Thick-knee, have well-camouflaged eggs, while those that nest in twig or grass nests placed in trees usually have blue or white eggs with brown blotches and other markings. Hole-nesting birds such as woodpeckers and kingfishers always have snow-white eggs.

Notes on the breeding habits of garden birds are included in the individual species descriptions that follow in the next chapter, including incubation and fledging periods.

The White-browed Robin-chat sometimes builds its nest in very close proximity to people; these youngsters are being raised in a plant bag.

CLUES TO BREEDING ACTIVITY

Many birds are secretive when nesting, not wanting to draw attention to the whereabouts of their eggs and young. However, there are many clues to indicate that birds are breeding in or near your garden.

Apart from a bird transporting nesting material, the most conspicuous sign of breeding is a bird carrying food as it flies purposefully in a given direction. This is a sure sign that it is feeding young or provisioning its mate on a nest. If a bird carrying food thinks you have seen it, it may take a circuitous route to its nest site or even abandon the feeding session and eat the food itself, hoping to go undetected on the next run.

Other evidence of breeding activity includes a bird stretching and preening vigorously, which may suggest that it has been sitting

With a beak full of fluffy Wild Camphor seedheads, this Brimstone Canary is undoubtedly en route to lining its nest.

motionless for a long period while incubating. If you see a bird carrying a small white purse in its bill, this is positive proof of an active nest, as this is a fecal sac being dumped away from the nest so that predators will not have a scent trail to follow. Not all birds do this, however. Hoopoes are notorious for fouling their own nests, and the high ammonia levels probably help to repel would-be predators.

You should also look out for birds flying up into the corners of your windows or searching under windowsills to gather cobwebs: sunbirds, flycatchers, batises, warblers and drongos are among the birds that use this silk in the construction of their nests. Similarly, birds gathering fluffy seedheads or picking up fallen feathers are sure to be lining a nest.

SUBURBAN BIRD TERRITORIES

The typical spacing of nest sites of six common bird species in a Western Cape suburb built alongside a greenbelt of strandveld vegetation. Plots in the suburb of Vermont are between 600 and 1,000m², so four or five stands are equivalent to about an acre (4,046m²). Species like Cape Robin-chats occur at higher densities in suburbs with their watered lawns, shrubberies and walls than they do in natural habitats. Others, like the Malachite Sunbird, are influenced by the availability and density of the nectar-bearing plants on which they feed.

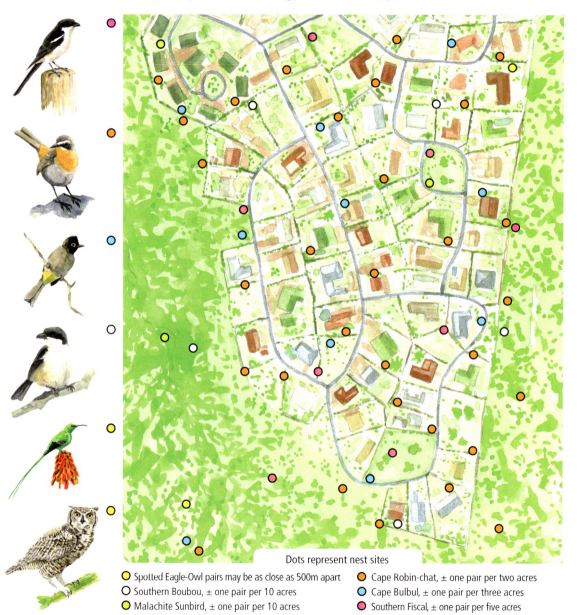

Dots represent nest sites

- ○ Spotted Eagle-Owl pairs may be as close as 500m apart
- ○ Southern Boubou, ± one pair per 10 acres
- ○ Malachite Sunbird, ± one pair per 10 acres
- ○ Cape Robin-chat, ± one pair per two acres
- ○ Cape Bulbul, ± one pair per three acres
- ○ Southern Fiscal, ± one pair per five acres

SEASONAL MIGRATION

Southern Africa's birds fall into three categories – residents, nomads and migrants. Resident birds occupy much the same area throughout the year and have a definite breeding season. Nomads are prone to erratic movements, usually associated with rainfall patterns. Migratory birds undertake predictable annual movements, often covering thousands of kilometres from one hemisphere to another.

Migratory birds can be further divided into three main groups. *Long-distance migrants* from the northern hemisphere are present from September to April, but do not breed here, e.g. the Barn Swallow, Spotted Flycatcher and Willow Warbler. *Intra-African migrants* come from other parts of the continent to breed here, such as the Greater Striped Swallow, Red-chested Cuckoo and Violet-backed Starling. *Altitudinal migrants* move from higher elevations to lower elevations with the seasons, e.g. the African Dusky Flycatcher and Red-capped Robin-chat.

Migration is a means for birds to increase their survival and reproductive rate by moving seasonally from one region to another. To put it in the simplest terms (although migration is complex and dynamic behaviour), birds that migrate are moving from a place where food is running out to a place where food is plentiful.

Virtually all of the species that migrate to southern Africa, whether from Europe, Asia or equatorial Africa, are insectivorous, or at least primarily so. They come here to feed on insects that occur in such abundance that the resident birds can consume only a small percentage of them: termites, grasshoppers and locusts, for example, experience huge population eruptions. Minuscule airborne midges and their relatives provide sustenance for millions of Barn Swallows as well as tens of thousands of other hirundines and swifts every summer. Conversely, the density of these aerial insects is so low in the dry winter months that only a few species of swallows and swifts can provide for themselves.

Licensed bird ringers capture and mark birds, such as this Greater Striped Swallow, with an individually numbered ring (leg tag), so that valuable valuable information on migratory movements can be obtained.

The most intriguing aspect of bird migration is *how* birds actually find their way to their destination. This is the focus of continuing research by ornithologists, as satellite technology allows us to build up an ever-clearer picture. Amazingly, a small bird such as the Spotted Flycatcher may breed in an English beech wood and then fly south to position itself in precisely the same shubbery in a Gauteng garden several years in succession. Birds that migrate after dark use sky polarisation patterns, noting the position of the setting sun, as well as constellations of stars, to chart their course. The Earth's magnetic field may also be a factor in how they orientate themselves.

As geolocators and satellite transmitters become ever smaller, and the methods of plotting bird movements become more precise, so the daily progress of individual migrants can be monitored. Migratory birds that traverse great distances pose enormous conservation challenges, because their wellbeing depends upon cooperation between various nations, and accurate data obtained on movements is of great importance when implementing appropriate conservation strategies.

Southern Boubou
Hermanus, Western Cape

101 GARDEN BIRDS

These are the birds most likely to appear in suburban gardens in the main towns and cities in southern Africa. This is both an identification guide and a source of interesting information on these familiar birds.

In selecting the 101 species that follow, an attempt has been made to be as representative of as many parts of the region as possible. Birds such as the Cape Robin-chat and Spotted Eagle-Owl occur in and around most of southern Africa, while others such as the Scaly-feathered Finch and Cape Sugarbird are restricted to specific regions, yet they are common and conspicuous garden birds within their comparatively small ranges. In several of the accounts, mention is made of similar species to which the featured bird is related or with which it might be confused.

The species are arranged so that similar birds are featured opposite or close to one another, rather than attempting to follow the sequence of current field guides and checklists, as these taxonomic arrangements are anyway in an unresolved state.

Where known, the longevity is given for each bird species. This information is based on data collected from bird-ringing studies co-ordinated by SAFRING (see p.186), and it will come as a surprise to most readers that a tiny Cape White-eye can live up to 12 years or that a Cape Robin-chat might reach the age of 17. However, the ages given are maximums, not averages, with most individuals not living for that period of time.

Average size is indicated at the top of each species account. The bird's silhouette is given relative to that of one of three well-known birds – the Cape Sparrow, Cape Turtle Dove or Helmeted Guineafowl – which should allow you to gauge their size in the field.

Cape Sparrow
14cm

Cape Turtle Dove
27cm

Helmeted Guineafowl
50cm

Ashy Flycatcher, Nelspruit, Mpumalanga

HADEDA IBIS

Bostrychia hagedash • **85cm**

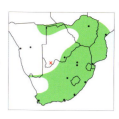

With its goose-shaped body, long, curved bill and raucous voice, the Hadeda is quite unmistakable. The sexes are alike. Individuals or small groups forage on lawns and in clearings, digging in the soil or searching among fallen leaves for invertebrates. Over the past few decades, the Hadeda's range and population have expanded greatly, and it now occurs throughout much of southern Africa except in the Kalahari and the driest parts of the Karoo.

Feeding: The long, curved bill is used to probe soft ground and to flick through leaf litter and compost heaps. Fat juicy grubs are its favoured prey, but earthworms, mole-crickets, cockroaches and snails also feature in its diet. Toads, frogs and lizards may be seized if the opportunity arises. In coastal areas the Hadeda feeds in the intertidal zone.

Breeding: The breeding cycle usually begins in September. Twigs are collected on the ground and arranged into a sparse bowl or platform in the fork of a tree, at a height of about 4–5m. The clutch of three eggs is incubated by both sexes for 25–28 days, while nestlings fledge at around 34 days.

Voice: The call is a raucous, honking 'ha-ha, ha-dee-dah', with a distinct tone of fear to it. Occasionally, small groups will engage in a discordant cacophony of alarm, from a rooftop or in low, circling flight. They often begin calling before dawn, waking people well before their alarm clocks are set to go off.

Lifespan: Ten years recorded, but probably able to reach at least 20.

Garden needs: Open lawns with some shady retreats and an accumulation of leaf litter where invertebrates can be found. Needs tall trees with high forks for nesting.

Similar species: The Glossy Ibis, which is restricted to wetlands, is much more slender. Other ibises in southern Africa are the African Sacred and near-endemic Southern Bald ibises.

The Hadeda extracts mole-crickets (**inset**) and other invertebrates from soft soil, finding sports fields and large lawns to be ideal foraging sites.

HELMETED GUINEAFOWL
Numida meleagris • **50cm**

With its polka-dotted plumage, rotund body and tiny head, this comical-looking bird has adapted well to human alteration of the landscape and is now more abundant in farmland than in its natural habitat. Gardens situated in new or outlying suburbs or homes adjacent to parks and golf courses are regularly visited by guineafowl, which may become quite tame and bold around people and domestic animals. Sexes are alike, but males usually have larger 'helmets'. Normally seen in flocks of 10 or more.

Feeding: Its diet consists of seeds, shoots, small bulbs and berries, as well as invertebrates such as termites, spiders and grasshoppers.

Breeding: At the end of winter, flocks break up as females choose mates from among the competing males. A pair may remain together for up to four years. Males may feed females during courtship and will defend them from rivals. A clutch of 6–18 eggs is laid in a shallow scrape lined with plant fibres and situated within tall rank grass or other cover. The female incubates her eggs for 26 days, and the chicks are able to flutter-fly by about 14 days. Those that are not picked off by predators remain together as a family group through winter.

Voice: A distinctive staccato cackle is the usual call, given in alarm at a potential predator or when settling at the night roost.

Lifespan: Fifteen years recorded in captivity.

Garden needs: Only likely to appear in larger open areas with good visibility. A scattering of grain will encourage guineafowl to visit open gardens, but this should not be done without careful consideration, as large numbers can become a nuisance, dominating other birds and damaging the surrounding vegetation.

Similar species: The Crested Guineafowl occurs in the forests of Zululand, northern Limpopo and Zimbabwe, but is unlikely to enter any garden.

The various races of Helmeted Guineafowl differ in the size and shape of the helmet-shaped casque, as well as the length of the gape wattles. Both male and female have these ornaments.

CAPE SPURFOWL
Pternistes capensis • 42cm

Under normal circumstances, spurfowl and francolins tend to be shy, nervous birds, but some species take advantage of easy food sources and can become tame. So it is that the Cape Spurfowl has become a regular visitor to open gardens in parts of the southern Cape. Coveys of up to a dozen birds gather wherever grain or seed is provided and frequently drink from birdbaths. Only the males have the distinctive long sharp spurs on their hind legs.

Feeding: Uses its powerful toes to rake through soil and sand for the seeds, small bulbs and fallen grain that make up its main diet. Snails, termites and ants are taken when available. In Strandveld, the berries of *Chrysanthemoides* are sometimes plucked directly from the bush.

Breeding: The breeding cycle usually begins in August. Rival males battle one another to secure dominance, with much chasing and kicking. The victorious cock circles the hen with drooped wings and raised back feathers, but if this does not lead to copulation he is willing to run the object of his desire into a corner. Up to 14 eggs are laid in a shallow scrape, hidden in the shade of a brush pile or shrub. The female incubates the eggs for 23 days; the hatchlings leave to follow their mother about 12 days after hatching.

Voice: Its usual call is a loud 'kaa-keek, kaa-keek, kaa-keeek', given at dawn and dusk from a prominent perch, but a tremulous horse-like whiny is also part of its repertoire.

Lifespan: No data, but probably reaches about eight years.

Garden needs: Open areas of lawn provide good foraging habitat, while sandy patches are used for dust bathing. Will visit birdbaths on a regular basis.

Similar species: The Red-billed Spurfowl visits gardens in towns such as Windhoek, Maun and Gaborone. The Natal Spurfowl may enter gardens in northeastern bushveld towns.

Youngsters **(above left)** maintain close contact with each other at all times. Only the male **(above right)** bears the strong leg spurs.

EGYPTIAN GOOSE
Alopochen aegyptiaca • 60–75cm (♂ larger)

This large waterfowl has adapted supremely well to human modification of the landscape. It has greatly expanded its range and numbers in recent decades with the proliferation of farm dams, ornamental water features and golf courses. It frequently visits or flies above suburban gardens, honking from rooftops and nesting in high places, sometimes competing with Spotted Eagle-Owls for suitable nest sites. The sexes are alike. Usually seen in pairs or family groups.

Feeding: Fully herbivorous, stripping seeds from grasses and sedges by combing sideways with its bill. Also nibbles on fresh grass and other plants and takes spilled grain seed from farmland, where large flocks may assemble.

Breeding: May breed in any month. Rival pairs are aggressive and demonstrative, engaging in noisy and prolonged disputes. Courtship display includes neck-stretching and wing-spreading. Nest sites are variable, sometimes on the ground among sedges near water, but also on high ledges on cliffs and buildings or on top of other birds' nests, especially those of the Hamerkop. The female incubates a clutch of 7–8 eggs for 28–30 days. After about 10 weeks the young are ready to leave the nest and are led to water by their parents. Those that are raised in high places jump to the ground, sometimes from great heights.

Voice: Strident honking and loud hissing if approached closely.

Lifespan: Fifteen years recorded.

Garden needs: Lawns and large ponds.

Similar species: None, but the the Yellow-billed Duck and exotic Mallard frequently occur alongside it in man-made ponds and dams on estates and in parks.

As soon as the goslings leave the nest, they are led to water by their parents (above). This bird's name is derived from its frequent appearance in ancient Egyptian hieroglyphics, as it was once common on the upper Nile River.

SPOTTED THICK-KNEE
Burhinus capensis • 43cm

This is a nocturnal bird of open country, known to many by its Afrikaans name *Dikkop* ('big head'). It relies on its cryptic mottled plumage to provide camouflage during the day. The huge yellow eyes are larger in relation to its head than those of any other bird. Occurs throughout southern Africa, where it has adapted to artificial habitats such as parks, sports fields and lawned estates, and is also seen on verges and in nearby gardens. By day, pairs favour shady spots, where they remain more or less motionless; after dark they forage on lawns, driveways and roads. Sexes alike.

Feeding: Insects such as beetles, termites and crickets are captured with a stab of the bill, following a brief chase. Also takes spiders, solifuges and millipedes in this way.

Breeding: The breeding cycle usually begins in September. Pairs may bond for life and occupy a territory throughout the year. Courtship displays occur after dark and include swooping flights and tail-fanning. No nest is made. Rather, a clutch of two camouflaged eggs is laid in a scrape on bare ground. Incubation lasts for about 26 days, with both parents sharing duties; the young are precocial, following their parents (but as yet unable to fly) for about eight weeks, during which time they are vulnerable to dogs and cats.

Voice: The night-time call is a loud, piercing whistle – 'pi-pi-pi-pipipipipipipipi' – building up to a crescendo then trailing off.

Lifespan: No data; the closely related Eurasian Stone-curlew *B. oedicnemus* is known to have reached 22 years.

Garden needs: Open areas in which to forage after dark, and quiet, lightly shaded areas away from pets in which to roost by day.

Similar species: The Water Thick-knee is a wetland bird that can occur on the fringes of man-made dams. These birds are also known as *Dikkops*.

The eggs and nestlings are superbly camouflaged, as is the incubating adult.

AFRICAN HARRIER-HAWK
Polyboroides typus • 63cm

This is a rather strange-looking bird of prey that bears physical similarities to goshawks, harriers and the large terrestrial Secretarybird. The head appears to be disproportionately small and the bare facial skin changes from pink to yellow depending on how agitated or aroused the bird is. Typically found in woodland areas, the harrier-hawk has adapted to habitat modification and may be seen in low, flapping flight above urban areas, frequently landing on rooftops to inspect eaves and cracks. Adults are predominantly blue-grey and the sexes are alike. Juveniles are sandy-brown with mottled plumage as they transition into adulthood.

Feeding: Nestling birds comprise its main diet; cavity breeders are not safe, as the harrier-hawk uses its long articulate legs to reach into holes and extract its prey. Swift and weaver colonies are often raided. The big raptor sometimes hangs upside down and uses its outstretched wings for balance as it tears open the nests. Young doves, mousebirds and sparrows are frequently taken, as well as the eggs of these and other species. Bats, lizards and frogs also feature on its menu.

Breeding: A large platform of sticks is placed high up in a tree fork, often in the tallest tree in the area. This nest may be used year after year and is refurbished prior to laying. Pairs sometimes take over the nest of a sparrowhawk or other raptor. The usual clutch is two eggs and it is mainly the female that incubates the eggs, for a period of 35 days. The nestlings remain in the nest for about 50 days and are fed only by the female who is provisioned by her mate.

Voice: A high-pitched 'sweeee-oh' is given in flight; the juvenile has a plaintive, drawn-out, begging whistle.

Lifespan: No information, but likely to reach 15 years.

Garden needs: Will prey on bats roosting in man-made bat boxes, as well as breeding swifts and weavers.

Similar species: Several other large hawks can occur in built-up areas. The Common Buzzard and Yellow-billed Kite are of a similar size to the African Harrier-Hawk.

The Gymnogene, as many still prefer to call it, specialises in pulling prey from holes and crevices – in this case a small bat **(left)**.

AFRICAN GOSHAWK

Accipiter tachiro • **36cm** (♂); **44cm** (♀)

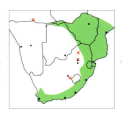

This agile and secretive raptor is often overlooked, but is common along the coast from Cape Town to East London and throughout most of KwaZulu-Natal, the lowveld and the bushveld. Although some people regard hawks as unwelcome garden visitors, they play a vital ecological role by preying on slow, weak or aged individuals. The female African Goshawk is considerably larger than the male, with brown rather than ash-grey upperparts; both have yellow eyes and a dusky-ochre cere that distinguishes the species from the Ovambo Sparrowhawk, Little Sparrowhawk and Shikra, all of which have a bright yellow cere. Usually seen singly or in pairs.

Feeding: Birds, mammals and lizards feature in this goshawk's diet. Prey is usually surprised in ambush and then pursued in flight. Being larger, female goshawks can overpower pigeons, turacos and squirrels, while the males take smaller prey, including bats, lizards and insects.

Breeding: The breeding cycle usually begins in October. The paired birds engage in territorial display flights, soaring high overhead while making a sharp 'chip!' call. A platform nest of twigs is built high in a leafy tree, typically on a branch away from the main trunk. The female incubates a clutch of 2–3 eggs for a 36-day period, during which time the male brings her food. Chicks remain in the nest for about four weeks before fledging.

Voice: A sharp 'chip!' call made while soaring high overhead; otherwise silent.

Lifespan: Eight years recorded, but closely related Eurasian Sparrowhawk *A. nisus* has reached over 20 years.

Garden needs: Well-wooded areas that provide cover for ambush hunting, and tall trees for nesting. Youngsters are especially prone to flying into windows. Will make regular use of a garden birdbath and will ambush smaller birds at bird tables.

Similar species: The Ovambo Sparrowhawk, Little Sparrowhawk and much larger Black Sparrowhawk also occur in suburban areas, often preying on smaller birds at garden feeding stations.

The male African Goshawk is pale grey above, while the considerably larger female has a dark brown back.

SPECKLED PIGEON
Columba guinea • **32cm**

This large rust-and-grey pigeon with spotted wings is a bird of mountains and rocky outcrops, but one that has adapted well to human alteration of the landscape. A familiar garden bird in Cape Town, Johannesburg, Bloemfontein, Gaborone and Windhoek. Houses and other buildings provide ideal nesting sites, similar enough to traditional cliff ledges, while farmlands provide abundant food and water. Usually seen in pairs or small groups, but larger flocks will gather at abundant food sources. Sexes are alike; the juvenile lacks the red facial skin.

Feeding: Forages on the ground for seeds of grasses and weeds, and eats fallen berries and figs. Large numbers may visit wheat fields, sunflower plantations and cereal crops.

Breeding: Breeding can occur at any time. Pairs sometimes nest less than 10m apart. The male performs a towering courtship display flight, gives a few sharp wingbeats as he gains height, then glides downwards in a spiral. A flimsy platform of dry twigs and grass stems is built on a ledge, in a hole in a wall, or under an eave. The parents take turns to incubate the clutch of two eggs for 15 days, and nestlings fledge at 20 days.

Voice: A deep, mellow cooing.

Lifespan: Ten years recorded.

Garden needs: Open areas for foraging and open-sided structures to serve as possible nest sites. Will feed from bird tables where seed and grain are provided. Drinks and bathes regularly, so will frequent birdbaths.

Similar species: The African Olive Pigeon and African Green Pigeon may visit gardens with figs or berry-producing trees.

The Speckled Pigeon may be confused with the alien Rock Pigeon (not pictured), a domesticated and feral bird found in large towns and cities. Confusingly, the Speckled was formerly known as the Rock Pigeon.

African Olive Pigeon

African Green Pigeon

LAUGHING DOVE
Streptopelia senegalensis • 23cm

This small, clay-coloured dove with grey-and-black wings is one of the most familiar birds in southern Africa, quite at ease feeding and nesting close to people. Usually seen singly or in small groups, often feeding in the company of other doves or smaller seedeaters. Occurs throughout the region and is absent only from dense forest and the highest windswept mountains. The sexes are alike. Juveniles have pale feather fringes that give them a scaly appearance.

Feeding: Forages in open areas, taking dry seeds from grasses and a variety of other plants, including agricultural crops. Also eats fallen berries and figs, as well as termites.

Breeding: Breeding can occur in any month, and pairs are thought to mate for life. The female builds a flimsy platform of thin twigs collected by her mate, usually quite low down in the fork of a shrub or tree. In the suburbs or on farms, she may build her nest on a window ledge or in a flowerpot. The parents take turns incubating the clutch of two eggs for a 13-day period, and the nestlings are brooded and fed for 14 days prior to fledging.

Voice: The call is a series of soft bubbling notes, reminiscent of laughter.

Lifespan: Eighteen years recorded.

Garden needs: Open areas for foraging and open-sided structures for nesting. Will feed from bird tables where seed and grain are provided. Drinks and bathes regularly, so is a frequent visitor at birdbaths.

Similar species: The Namaqua Dove can be a common garden bird in the drier western half of the region, sometimes ranging east into Gauteng and down to the southern Cape.

Namaqua Dove

Laughing Doves frequently sun themselves, perhaps as a way of exposing feather and skin parasites that are forced to move off, or die.

RED-EYED DOVE

Streptopelia semitorquata • **33cm**

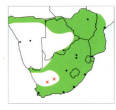

The largest of the ring-necked doves, this is a bulky pinkish-grey bird with a noticeably pale forecrown. The eyes are dark orange, surrounded by fleshy dark red eye rings. Usually seen alone or in pairs, but up to a dozen may gather at an abundant food source. Often seen in the company of other dove species at food and water. The sexes are alike. Juveniles are lighter than the adults, with pale fringes to their feathers.

Feeding: The seeds of grasses and crops make up its main diet. Also takes seeds from alien acacias and pines and the berries of trees such as *Trema* and *Gymnosporea*. Sedge bulbs and crops are eaten on the ground.

Breeding: Breeding can occur in any month. Pairs remain within a home territory and may mate for life. After courtship and mating, the male collects small twigs, typically breaking them off trees rather than collecting them from the ground. He gives them to the female, who uses them to build a platform, which she lines with softer plant material. Both parents help to incubate the clutch of two eggs for 16 days. Nestlings leave the nest after about two weeks.

Voice: The call is a series of deep, rhythmic, cooing sounds – 'krooooooo-kroo', with variations on the theme. Harsh growling notes are given during courtship.

Lifespan: Seven years recorded.

Garden needs: Open areas and a regular supply of seed or water. Will feed on seed and grain from bird tables. Drinks and bathes regularly, so will frequent birdbaths.

Most members of the genus *Streptopelia* are distinguished by a black neck collar (**above**). In courtship flight the male flies up high then glides down (**left**), often giving sharp wing flaps. He inflates his throat and bobs his head, then preens the female's head before mounting her.

Similar species: The African Mourning Dove is a common garden bird in Maun and Victoria Falls, as well as some towns in South Africa's Limpopo province.

African Mourning Dove

CAPE TURTLE DOVE

Streptopelia capicola • **27cm**

Best known for its rhythmic 'work har-der, work har-der' call, which is a familiar and evocative sound across most of southern Africa. This is a medium-sized dove with a distinctive neck collar and small dark eyes that lack fleshy eye rings. Usually seen alone or in pairs, but large flocks can gather at water sources in semi-desert areas or on farmland. Often in the company of other dove species at food and water. Sexes are alike. Juveniles are paler than the adults, with pale fringes to their feathers.

Feeding: Consumes mainly grass and millet seeds, and those of other crops. Also takes seeds from alien acacias and pines and the berries of *Searsia* and alien *Lantana* and *Pyracantha*.

Breeding: Can breed at any time of year. Pairs mate for life and stay in their home territory year-round. The male performs a towering courtship flight, ascending with clapping wings and then gliding down in a wide arc. Prior to mating he inflates his throat and bobs his head while uttering a series of harsh cooing sounds. The female uses thin twigs collected by her mate to build a flimsy platform nest in the fork of a shrub or tree. Both parents incubate the clutch of two eggs for a 14-day period, and the nestlings are brooded and fed for 16 days prior to fledging.

Voice: Gives a clear, three-syllabled 'work har-der, work har-der' call from a high perch.

Lifespan: Thirty-five years recorded!

Garden needs: Open areas and a regular supply of seeds or water. Will feed from bird tables where seed and grain are provided. Drinks and bathes regularly, so will frequent birdbaths.

Similar species: The shy Lemon Dove may occur in wooded gardens around Durban and Nelspruit. There is also a small population at Kirstenbosch.

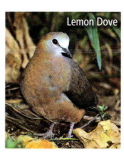

Lemon Dove

In the dry Kalahari and Karoo, large flocks of Cape Turtle Doves may gather to drink, sometimes at swimming pools!

BURCHELL'S COUCAL

Centropus burchellii • 40cm

Best known for its liquid bubbling call, like the sound of water being poured slowly from a long-necked bottle. This is a large but quite secretive bird that forages in dense thickets and is seemingly more at ease clambering from place to place than it is in flight. More or less restricted to South Africa, but absent only from the dry central Karoo and Kalahari. Usually seen alone and often most active just before and after rain. Sometimes mobbed by gangs of small birds. Sexes alike, but the female is larger.

Feeding: Stalks and ambushes a wide variety of animals, which it seizes and shakes with its large hooked bill. Frequently takes bird nestlings and eggs, as well as lizards, small snakes, chameleons, rodents, frogs, toads, spiders and insects. Usually swallows prey whole.

Breeding: The breeding cycle generally begins in October. Unusually, it is the female that advertises the territory, which she does by giving the bubbling call. This interesting role-reversal suggests a polyandrous mating system. In courtship, the male offers a food gift to the female prior to mating. The male makes an untidy rugby ball-shaped nest. This loosely woven oval of dry grass is lined with softer plant material and placed deep within a dense bush. Parents take turns to incubate the clutch of four eggs, and the young leave the nest at between two and three weeks.

Voice: The liquid bubbling 'bub, bub-bubububububububub' call is given most often at dusk and dawn, or throughout the day in rainy weather.

Lifespan: Just over three years recorded, but probably reaches at least 10 years.

Garden needs: Requires thickets in which to hunt and hide. May inhabit an artificial wetland.

Similar species: The Senegal Coucal may occupy thickets in gardens in Harare, Bulawayo, Victoria Falls and Maun.

The juvenile coucal (**above left**) has a patchy hood and is strongly barred. Burchell's Coucal takes a wide variety of prey items, including reptiles such as the Vine Snake (**above right**).

GREY GO-AWAY-BIRD

Corythaixoides concolor • **48cm**

Short on colour but not in personality, this demonstrative and highly vocal bird usually goes about in pairs or small groups. Formerly restricted to thorny savanna in the bushveld and lowveld, it has extended its range southwards onto the highveld, where alien tree species and suburban gardens now provide suitable habitat and food. The name 'go-away-bird' is imitative of its explosive call. The sexes are alike.

Feeding: Berries and small fruits of trees such as *Ziziphus*, *Euclea* and *Diospyros* predominate in its diet, but it also relishes buds, flowers and nectar. May raid peach orchards, and favours the berries of invasive Mulberry *Morus nigra* and Syringa *Melia azederach*, no doubt helping to spread these aliens. Eats termites whenever they are available.

Breeding: Breeding can occur at any time of year. Pairs engage in courtship feeding prior to mating. A flimsy saucer-shaped nest of dry twigs is placed in the centre of a thorny tree or, if that is not available, in a leafy tree or cluster of mistletoe. Both sexes help to incubate the clutch of three eggs for about 28 days. The young leave the nest some 20 days later, not yet able to fly.

Voice: One of the first birds to take fright at the approach of humans or predators; its harsh 'gwaaay' call led frustrated hunters to dub it the 'go-away-bird'.

Lifespan: Nine years recorded.

Garden needs: Fruit-bearing plants for sustenance and thorn trees in which to nest. Quick to visit food tables where pawpaws, bananas and other soft fruits are provided. Drinks and bathes frequently, so will visit birdbaths regularly.

Similar species: None.

Because of its size, the Grey Go-away-bird often dominates other birds at feeding tables and birdbaths.

PURPLE-CRESTED TURACO
Tuaraco porphyreolophus • 42cm

This glamorous multicoloured bird occurs in the warmer eastern lowveld and coastal regions, where it inhabits riverine forest and thicket as well as wooded gardens in towns such as Durban, Pietermaritzburg, Nelspruit and Harare. Usually seen in pairs or family groups, drawing attention with its hoarse barking call. The spectacular crimson flight feathers are fully visible only in flight. The sexes are alike, but young birds lack the red eye wattles.

Feeding: Figs and berries from trees such as *Trichelia*, *Anthocleista*, *Harpephyllum* and *Antidesma* make up its main diet. Also eats the buds and flowers of certain plants, and relishes the grape-sized fruits of *Clivia*. Berries are plucked from the ends of branches and swallowed whole. Winged termites may be hawked in flight.

Breeding: The breeding cycle usually begins in October, with rival males challenging and chasing one another. Pairs may be faithful for life. A flimsy platform of small twigs is built within a dense or thorny tree, usually well hidden. The clutch of 2–3 eggs is incubated for 22 days by both parents. Nestlings leave the nest at about three weeks, before they are able to fly.

Voice: Gives a loud barking 'kok-kok-kok-kok' from treetops, often rising to a wild crescendo.

Lifespan: No data, but a captive Knysna Turaco *T. corythaix* lived for 10 years.

Garden needs: Large evergreen trees that provide cover as well as food. Will feed from bird tables where fruit is provided. Drinks and bathes often, and will visit a shaded birdbath regularly.

Similar species: The Knysna Turaco (featured opposite) may occur alongside the Purple-crested in and around Durban.

With its distinctive barking call, iridescent head feathers and crimson primaries (visible when the wing is open), the Purple-crested Turaco is one of the region's most striking birds.

KNYSNA TURACO

Tauraco corythaix • **46cm**

This glorious, mostly moss-green bird occurs in the Eastern Cape and southern KwaZulu-Natal, where it inhabits temperate forest as well as wooded gardens in towns such as Knysna, Plettenberg Bay and East London. Usually seen in pairs or family groups. The spectacular crimson flight feathers are fully visible only in flight. The sexes are alike, but young birds lack the red eye wattles. Formerly known as the Knysna Lourie. A separate population (race *phoebus*) occurs in montane forests in eastern Mpumalanga and Limpopo and may visit gardens in towns such as Barberton and Tzaneen.

Feeding: Figs and berries from trees such as the Wild Plum *Harpephyllum caffrum* (see below), *Ekebergia*, *Sideroxylon* and *Pittosporum* make up its main diet. Also eats the buds and flowers of certain plants, and relishes the grape-sized fruits of *Clivia*. Plucks berries from the ends of branches and swallows them whole. May hawk winged termites in flight.

Breeding: Breeding begins in September, with rival males challenging and chasing one another. Pairs are thought to mate for life. A flimsy platform of small twigs is built in a dense tree or tangled creeper, usually well hidden. Two eggs are incubated for 23 days by both parents. Nestlings leave the nest at about three weeks, before they are able to fly.

Voice: Gives a series of growling notes and explosive rasping cries.

Lifespan: At least 10 years in captivity.

Garden needs: Large evergreen trees that provide cover as well as food. Will feed from bird tables where fruit is provided. Will visit a shaded birdbath regularly.

Similar species: The Livingstone's Turaco occurs in far northern Zululand and the Eastern Highlands of Zimbabwe, where it may enter wooded gardens in Mutare.

In its relatively small range, the Knysna Turaco is among the most celebrated of garden visitors.

Harpephyllum caffrum

RED-CHESTED CUCKOO

Cuculus solitarius • 28cm

This secretive bird is rarely seen but is nevertheless well known for its strident repetitive call – 'piet-my-vrou!' Occurs over the eastern half of southern Africa as well as in the southern Cape. Males call from favoured perches, usually hidden below the crown of a tall tree. A summer migrant, arriving in early September and leaving in April. In body shape and flight, this cuckoo resembles a small hawk.

Feeding: Eats mainly caterpillars, but also takes katydids, spiders, snails and slugs. Finds prey by searching through foliage, and hawks winged termites from the air.

Breeding: The male occupies a territory and calls persistently to attract females and keep other males out. Visiting females are presented with a caterpillar prior to mating. Rather than build a nest or incubate their own eggs, cuckoos parasitise the nests of other birds. The most common host is the Cape Robin-chat, but Cape Wagtail and Karoo Thrush nests are also frequently parasitised. Females must be sly and persistent as they go about depositing one egg at a time into various nests, while also removing one of the host's eggs. Up to 20 eggs are laid in this way per season. The cuckoo egg has a shorter incubation period (12 days) than that of the host (16 days), so it hatches earlier and the cuckoo chick evicts the remaining eggs.

Voice: The male's three-noted call can continue for hours, sometimes throughout the night. The female gives an excited cackling call, probably given prior to mating. Typically ceases calling by February.

Lifespan: No data, but the oldest Common Cuckoo *C. canorus* reached seven years.

Garden needs: Tall trees and wooded areas. Wild Peach *Kiggelaria africana* may host large numbers of caterpillars that attract cuckoos.

Similar species: The Common Cuckoo is a non-breeding summer migrant from Eurasia and is mostly silent when in southern Africa.

The male Red-chested Cuckoo calls from the upper canopy of tall trees. The juvenile (inset), here being fed by a Karoo Thrush foster parent, has a charcoal back and throat.

DIEDERIK CUCKOO

Chrysococcyx caprius • 18cm

This small, glossy green cuckoo occurs over most of southern Africa, being absent only from the driest parts of the Nama Karoo. Arrives from equatorial Africa in September and departs in March. The copper-coloured female is furtive and rarely seen, but the vociferous male is not at all shy. He perches openly, often on wire fences, and is frequently seen being chased by weavers. Young birds have a distinctive orange bill.

Feeding: Caterpillars form the bulk of its diet, but it may take other insects from foliage and will hawk winged termites. Grasps and shakes caterpillars before swallowing them.

Breeding: The male calls persistently from his territory to attract females and keep competitors away. Females receive a caterpillar gift prior to mating. Like the Red-chested Cuckoo, the Diederik Cuckoo parasitises the nests of other birds, in this case those of weavers, bishops and sparrows. Egg-laying females deposit a single egg at a time into various nests, removing one of the host's eggs. Up to 24 eggs are laid in this way per season. The cuckoo egg incubates for 12 days, whereas the host bird's eggs incubate for longer (14 days for weavers). When it hatches, the cuckoo chick evicts the remaining eggs or nestlings. Colonial weavers are particularly aggressive in defending their nests from cuckoos.

Voice: Its name derives from its familiar, plaintive, whistled 'dee-dee-diderik' call.

Lifespan: Six years recorded.

Garden needs: Is attracted to gardens where weavers are nesting. The Wild Peach *Kiggelaria africana* hosts large numbers of caterpillar prey.

Look out for Diederik Cuckoos around active weaver colonies **(left)** during early summer, when females sneak into the woven nests to lay their eggs.

Similar species: Klaas's Cuckoo regularly visits well-wooded gardens from Cape Town to Durban, and in the eastern half of the region.

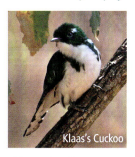

Klaas's Cuckoo

SPOTTED EAGLE-OWL
Bubo africanus • 45cm

This owl has distinctive ear tufts that give it a cat-like silhouette. The sexes are alike. Usually seen singly or in pairs on rooftops or streetlights at dusk, it often hunts along roads and in illuminated gardens. More often heard than seen, it gives a soft, deep call. The finely barred chest distinguishes it from the larger Cape Eagle-Owl, which is a bird of boulder-strewn mountains and cliffs.

Over most of its range, the Spotted Eagle-Owl has yellow eyes **(above)**, but birds in the southwestern Cape may have darker, orange eyes **(left)**, leading to confusion with the larger Cape Eagle-Owl, a shy mountain bird that rarely hunts around towns.

Feeding: Hunts rodents and small birds, but also takes large numbers of beetles and other invertebrates. Despite claims to the contrary, its feet are small and not powerful enough to tackle domestic cats or small dogs, although it may attack them in defence of its young. Hunts from a perch, dropping silently onto its prey or swooping in to attack from behind. Regurgitates pellets of undigested materials (bones, fur and beetle shells) at the roost.

Breeding: Pairs probably mate for life and occupy a territory throughout the year, calling most frequently prior to breeding. The male presents his partner with food before copulation. A clutch of 2–3 eggs is laid low down in a rock crevice, quarry or gaping tree fork. Will also nest on a sheltered ledge or in an owl box. The female incubates the eggs for 32 days. Young move off the 'nest' after about three weeks, before they are able to fly. Adults can be very protective, defending their nest sites with bill snapping and readily striking people and dogs.

Voice: Gives a deep, double-noted hoot – 'huuu-huuuuuuu' – often in duet. The female has a deeper voice than her mate. Calls most vigorously at dawn and dusk.

Lifespan: Fifteen years recorded.

Garden needs: A nest box or ledge for breeding. An outdoor light will attract nocturnal insects to provide possible prey.

Similar species: The much larger Verreaux's Eagle-Owl may visit gardens on farms in bushveld regions.

WESTERN BARN OWL
Tyto alba • 32cm

This owl is strictly nocturnal and rarely seen, but its high-pitched screechy call is frequently heard. Its white face and body and long, spindly legs give it a ghost-like appearance, and it features in fables and folklore across its wide global range. It gets the name Barn Owl from its habit of roosting and nesting in wooden barns on farms, where it is a frequent presence, feeding on rats and mice attracted to grain.

Feeding: Hunts rodents by coursing low over grassland and scrub, dropping silently, feet-first, onto its prey. Small birds, shrews, geckos, frogs and scorpions are also taken this way, but bats are captured in flight. Regurgitates undigested material (like bones, bird beaks and fur) at the roost site. These pellets can be examined to determine prey species.

Breeding: A pair occupy a territory throughout the year, finding a cavity of some kind in which to lay eggs and raise young. Frequently uses artificial structures, especially barns, warehouses, chimneys in ruined buildings, mineshafts and grain silos. Natural sites include large tree holes, dongas, rock faces, abandoned Hamerkop nests and the thatch-like frond masses of tall palms. The nest site is also used as a day roost and can be occupied for decades. The usual clutch size is 5–6 eggs, but this may increase to 19 eggs during a rodent population explosion. The female incubates her eggs for about 30 days, laying at three-day intervals so that the nestlings fledge at staggered intervals. Thus they differ greatly in size.

Voice: A hissing screech, given in flight.

Lifespan: Fifteen years recorded.

Garden needs: A suitably constructed nest box may attract this owl.

Similar species: The similarly sized African Wood Owl occurs in well-wooded suburbs in Cape Town, as well as in towns such as Durban, Knysna, Nelspruit and Harare.

Warwick Tarboton

African Wood Owl

The Western Barn Owl occurs on every continent except Antarctica, and there are numerous regional races. Members of Tytonidae, the family to which it belongs, differ from typical owls (Strigidae) in having small dark eyes set in a facial disc.

AFRICAN GREY HORNBILL
Lophoceros nasutus • **46cm**

This is a bird of thorn savanna and open woodland, visiting gardens in towns such as Pretoria, Hoedspruit, Gaborone and Bulawayo. Depending on rainfall patterns, these hornbills may be seasonal visitors to Fourways, Randburg and other parts of Johannesburg. Usually in pairs or family groups. The lovely whistled call is often heard before the birds themselves are seen. In females the upper mandible of the bill is cream, while the bill tip is burgundy.

Feeding: Invertebrates and berries make up the bulk of this hornbill's diet, but geckos and others lizards are also taken.

Breeding: Lays 3–4 eggs in a natural tree cavity or woodpecker's hole. The male seals the female inside, using mud or dung for the job. He then provisions her with food throughout the 24–27-day incubation period, until she breaks out with her young. Nest holes are typically 2–4m above the ground. May also use a nest box.

Voice: The plaintive, drawn-out, whistling 'pee-pee-pee-pipipeeuw' is often heard before the birds are seen.

Lifespan: Likely to reach at least 20 years.

Garden needs: May visit bird tables where fruit is provided, and will drink and bathe in hot weather. *Ficus*, *Ekebergia* and *Commiphora* are among the fruits relished.

Similar species: The Southern Yellow-billed and Southern Red-billed hornbills visit gardens in northern bushveld regions, while Monteiro's Hornbill is a familiar bird around Windhoek.

The female (**above**) has a cream-coloured bill with a burgundy tip, while the male's (**left**) is dark grey with a longer casque on the upper mandible.

Southern Yellow-billed Hornbill

TRUMPETER HORNBILL
Bycanistes bucinator • 50–65cm

 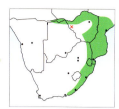

This large and impressive hornbill will visit gardens in the eastern coastal districts, where it is a familiar visitor in places like Port Edward, Kloof, Umhlanga, Amanzimtoti and Mtunzini. However, it may also appear seasonally in towns such as Nelspruit and Hoedspruit. Usually seen in pairs or small groups, maintaining contact with plaintive calls, but may gather in larger flocks of up to 50. The male has a much larger bill casque than the female. This species is prone to fighting its own reflection in windowpanes.

Feeding: Feeds mostly on berries and figs, often spending hours in a single tree. Relishes the fruit of all *Ficus* species, as well as *Ekebergia*, *Rauvolfia*, *Trichilia* and *Berchemia*; will break open the woody pods of *Afzelia quanzensis* to extract the seeds. Also eats the fleshy outer skin of cycad seeds. In the breeding season its diet includes winged termites, caterpillars, paper-wasp larvae, millipedes and the eggs of other birds.

Breeding: Defends its nesting cavity vigorously, but ranges far and wide when not breeding. The male cements the female into the nest while she incubates her clutch of 2–3 eggs. She remains walled in for the entire 50-day fledging period too – a total of nearly three months. The male collects and brings food to his partner and the nestlings, sometimes aided by a helper, usually one of their offspring from a previous brood.

Voice: Croaking, braying sounds and a nasal wailing call, like that of a crying baby.

Lifespan: Twenty-one years recorded.

Garden needs: Large fruit-bearing trees. May take mealworms and bonemeal.

Similar species: The smaller Crowned Hornbill may visit coastal gardens from Port Elizabeth to Mtunzini. It is also occasionally seen in bushveld towns such as Hoedspruit.

The male Trumpeter Hornbill (above) sports a large casque on the top of his bill, while the female's (left) is shorter; the purpose of these casques in uncertain, but they may amplify the sound of calls.

Crowned Hornbill

AFRICAN HOOPOE

Upupa africana • 26cm

This dove-sized bird, with its unique fan-shaped crest of head feathers, occurs throughout southern Africa, avoiding only forests, extremely arid areas and high mountains. Is usually seen on the ground, singly or in pairs, walking about in a jerky bobbing manner in search of food. Sexes are similar. The monotonous call is familiar to many people. With its broad white-spotted wings, it resembles a massive butterfly in flight.

Feeding: Captures beetles, termites, other insects and spiders by probing the soil and leaf litter or by flicking over dry animal dung. Often digs into soft soil with its long bill, pulling out insect larvae and earthworms.

Breeding: Pairs occupy a home range throughout the year, advertising their presence with regular calling. Nests in a cavity of some kind: natural tree holes, especially those in old oaks and willows, are favoured, but will also use dongas, stone walls, old buildings, rubble heaps or holes in the ground. The female incubates a clutch of 4–6 eggs for 15–16 days. The male feeds his mate at the nest and joins her in feeding the nestlings during the month-long fledging period. Because the young defecate inside the nest cavity, it becomes extremely foul smelling.

Voice: Gives a soft, far-carrying 'hoop-huu' territorial call, from which it gets its name. Often calls monotonously for lengthy periods, being especially vocal prior to breeding. The incubating female and young make a hissing snake-like sound that may be a defensive strategy.

Lifespan: Ten years recorded.

Garden needs: Lawns provide ideal foraging conditions; has adapted well to urban areas with parks and sports fields. May breed in a nest box or stone wall.

Similar species: None.

A loose stone wall like the one shown here may provide a suitable nesting site for the African Hoopoe.

GREEN WOOD-HOOPOE
Phoeniculus purpureus • 32–34cm

The Green Wood-hoopoe is hard to ignore. As if the shimmering indigo-and-emerald plumage and dagger-shaped scarlet bill were not enough, these gregarious birds are noisy and engage in synchronised bouts of acrobatics. Invariably seen in loud family groups foraging low down in trees or hanging from higher branches. Sexes are similar. Occurs in the warmer and wetter eastern parts of South Africa, but has become common in Johannesburg, where the wooded suburbs provide the ideal habitat.

Feeding: Preys on beetle larvae and all manner of insects, along with spiders, geckos, tree frogs and, sometimes, the eggs of small birds. Uses its long bill to probe crevices, cracks and bark in tree trunks and branches. Also takes nectar of *Erythrina*, *Aloe* and others.

Breeding: Family groups occupy and defend a home range throughout the year, calling regularly to advertise their presence and engaging in territorial disputes with their neighbours. A clutch of 3–4 eggs is laid in a natural tree cavity or a hole made by a woodpecker or barbet (these excavators often being driven away from their own homes); less often they nest in a pipe or a hole in a wall. The female incubates her eggs for 18 days, being fed during this period by her mate and helpers – offspring from previous broods. The chicks fledge after about 30 days. The nest cavity smells foul because the young defecate inside it.

Voice: All members of the family unit give a wild cackling chorus, accompanied by head bowing and tail swaying. Interactions between neighbouring families can be intense.

Lifespan: Fourteen years recorded

Garden needs: Requires large older trees, with dead and decaying branches in which to forage. Families may roost in chimneys and roof eaves and may occupy a nest box. Will visit bird tables for mealworms and bonemeal.

Similar species: The Common Scimitarbill may visit gardens in towns surrounded by dry bushveld, such as Kimberley and Gaborone.

Green Wood-hoopoes frequently visit feeding stations **(left)** where bonemeal or mealworms have been provided.

BLACK-COLLARED BARBET

Lybius torquatus • **20cm**

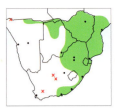

This bold and gregarious bird makes itself known with its strident vocalisations. The name 'black-collared' has puzzled people for generations, as its flame-red head is a much more distinctive trait. As it happens, there are other members of the genus further north in Africa, with fully red heads, and they have this name. Usually seen in family groups of 3–9, perched together in treetops. The sexes are alike.

Feeding: Eats mainly soft fruit and berries but also takes insects, especially winged termites. Loves ripe figs and takes many berries, including those of *Dovyalis*, *Cussonia*, *Syzygium*, *Sideroxylon* and *Diospyros*. Readily takes apples and other fruit placed on feeding tables. The nectar of *Aloe*, *Erythrina* and *Schotia* flowers is sometimes taken.

Breeding: Helpers from previous broods assist the breeding pair. The family defends a territory by calling from high perches. The mated pair begins, and other members of the family join in. They excavate a nest hole in soft wood, usually a dead branch, but also nest in logs of sisal or willow. Both sexes, and sometimes the helpers, take turns to incubate the clutch of 3–4 eggs for 18 days, and chicks fledge after about 34 days. They are aggressive towards the Lesser Honeyguide, a persistent brood parasite.

Voice: Male and female give a loud, bubbling 'two-puddely, two-puddely, two-puddely' duet, with much head bobbing and swaying; also various harsh, grating alarm calls.

Lifespan: Six years recorded, but probably lives to at least 10.

Garden needs: Dead branches with a diameter of more than 15cm, or nest logs. Fruit- and berry-producing trees.

Similar species: The White-eared Barbet is a regular garden visitor along much of the KwaZulu-Natal coast, while Whyte's Barbet occurs in some Harare gardens.

The Lesser Honeyguide (**inset**) is a brood parasite of Black-collared Barbet nests, laying its eggs to be tended by barbets. Barbets are wary of honeyguides and noisy battles take place between the two species.

CRESTED BARBET
Trachyphonus vaillantii • **24cm**

 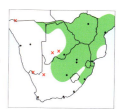

With its spangled yellow plumage and spiky crest of head feathers, this jaunty bird is conspicuous wherever it occurs, including suburban gardens around Johannesburg, Pretoria, Durban, Bloemfontein and Harare. Usually seen singly or in pairs, calling monotonously from an exposed high perch or rooftop. The sexes are alike. Regularly visits feeding tables where fruit is provided, dominating most other birds.

Feeding: Insects such as beetles, termites and grasshoppers feature prominently in its diet and are taken on the ground. Snails are bashed against stones or paving before being swallowed. Ripe figs and berries from trees such as *Kiggelaria*, *Ekebergia* and *Halleria* are taken. Will also visit peach and apricot orchards.

Breeding: A pair mates for life and defends a territory throughout the year, calling regularly to advertise their presence. The nest hole is also used as a night roost and is defended aggressively against other hole-nesting birds. Breeding holes are excavated in the decaying wood of a dead branch, a natural cavity or a sisal log wired to a tree. Both sexes help to incubate the clutch of 3–4 eggs for 15 days, and the young fledge after about 29 days.

Voice: Its monotonous 'trrrrrrrrrrrrrrrrrrrrrrrrrrr' trill is often likened to the sound of an old-fashioned alarm clock.

Lifespan: Seven years recorded.

Garden needs: Dead branches (with a diameter of more than 20cm) and sisal nesting logs provide breeding opportunities. Will visit berry-producing trees and comes readily to apples and other fruit placed on feeding tables.

Similar species: None.

The Crested Barbet is an excitable bird, raising its crest feathers and flashing its scarlet rump when calling or interacting with other birds.

ACACIA PIED BARBET

Tricholaema leucomelas • **17cm**

This stocky, sparrow-sized bird can be recognised by its oversized bill and scarlet forecrown. Sexes are alike. It is most likely to visit gardens in semi-arid areas, being drawn to water and fruit. Usually seen singly, but associates with other species at bird tables and birdbaths. In recent years, its range has extended west with the spread of Australian *Acacia* trees. The distinctive nasal call carries for some distance, and this bird is heard more often than it is seen.

Feeding: Berries of the parasitic mistletoes *Loranthus* and *Viscum* are much favoured, as are ripe figs; also feeds on the berries of trees such as *Boscia*, *Searsia* and *Euclea*.

Breeding: Pairs defend a breeding territory, engaging in courtship behaviour that includes head bobbing and swaying, while calling in duet. A nesting cavity is excavated in a dead branch of a tree or the stem of a large *Aloe* or *Agave*, both sexes sharing the job. In the absence of a suitable tree hole, it may breed in the mud-pellet nest of a swallow. The clutch of three eggs is incubated for two weeks by both sexes and must be defended against the Lesser Honeyguide, which is a brood parasite. The young fledge after about 35 days.

Voice: Gives two distinctive calls. The most frequent is a loud nasal 'njeehp-njeehp'. Also gives a softer 'hoop, hoop, hoop' that is very similar to the call of the African Hoopoe.

Lifespan: Eleven years recorded.

Garden needs: Berry-bearing shrubs for food and dead tree branches or sisal logs in which to nest. Will visit birdbaths in hot weather.

Similar species: The tiny Red-fronted Tinkerbird visits coastal gardens from East London to Empangeni, while the Yellow-fronted Tinkerbird may occur in Pretoria, Bulawayo and Harare gardens.

The Acacia Pied Barbet is usually seen singly or in pairs, typically calling from the top or outer branches of a tree.

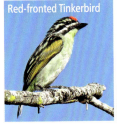

Red-fronted Tinkerbird

RED-THROATED WRYNECK

Jynx ruficollis • **19**cm

With its streaky brown plumage resembling the bark of a tree and providing it with superb camouflage, this peculiar bird would be easy to overlook if it didn't have such a persistent and strident call. The Red-throated Wryneck is usually seen singly or in pairs, calling repetitively from an exposed perch or foraging quietly on the ground. Sexes are alike, with a rich brick-red throat and upper breast; the juvenile has only a faint rusty wash on the throat.

Feeding: Feeds on ants and their eggs, foraging mostly on the ground. Scratches the soil, gathering prey with its long sticky tongue.

Breeding: Pairs occupy a territory throughout the year. A clutch of 3–4 eggs is laid in a cavity, usually the disused nest hole of a woodpecker or barbet. These wrynecks often also nest in hollow metal fence posts or in nest boxes. Frequently challenged by kingfishers, starlings and barbets that wish to occupy the nest hole. Both sexes share incubation duties for 13 days, guarding against parasitism by the Lesser Honeyguide, and the young fledge after about 25 days.

Voice: Calls from a favoured perch such as a telephone pole or treetop. The nasal 'quee-quee-quee-quee' is not unlike the sound of a plastic bath toy being squeezed.

Lifespan: No data, but a Eurasian Wryneck *J. torquilla* reached 10 years.

Garden needs: Dead branches host arboreal ants and provide nesting opportunities. Make sure the nest box or log has a hole in it, as the bird is unable to excavate its own. Lawns and bare ground are used for foraging.

The name 'wryneck' comes from the strange habit these birds have of tilting and twisting their neck. Wrynecks are related to woodpeckers but lack the stiff tail feathers and powerful bill for excavating into solid wood.

Similar species: The Olive Woodpecker is an occasional visitor to coastal gardens from Cape Town to Durban, and those of towns close to the eastern escarpment.

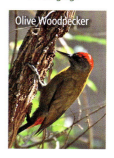

Olive Woodpecker

CARDINAL WOODPECKER
Dendropicos fuscescens • 15cm

This is the smallest woodpecker in southern Africa, occurring over most of the region apart from the treeless parts of the Karoo. Usually seen singly, but sometimes forages in trees with other insectivorous birds such as tits and flycatchers. Often first detected by its characteristic tapping, as it pecks into wood for food. Males differ from females in having a scarlet hind crown. The larger Golden-tailed Woodpecker also has streaked, not spotted or barred, underparts but the male of this bulbul-sized bird has a red moustachial stripe.

Feeding: Taps and bores into branches in search of the larvae of beetles and other insects, pecking at various angles and using its barbed tongue to extract the grubs. Often hangs upside down from small branches, stems and dry seed pods. Feeds opportunistically on spiders and winged termites.

Breeding: Pairs occupy a territory year-round, excavating a nest hole on the underside of a dead branch or sisal nesting log. The female lays two eggs on a bed of wood chips, and both sexes help to incubate them for 12 days. The young fledge after about 27 days.

Voice: The call is a high-pitched rattle, given by both sexes. Also gives a soft but distinctive drumming 'grrrrru', made by rapidly striking the same point on a dead branch. Rival pairs engage in more strident vocal battles.

Lifespan: No data, but similar woodpeckers live about 11 years.

Garden needs: Dead branches, especially thinner twigs, and trees with woody seed pods will attract this little woodpecker.

Similar species: The Golden-tailed Woodpecker is a larger bird of the warmer, northern and eastern parts of the region; sometimes seen in Gauteng gardens.

The Cardinal Woodpecker is often seen hanging upside down from a twig or tapping a dead branch in search of beetle larvae.

Golden tailed Woodpecker

BROWN-HOODED KINGFISHER

Halcyon albiventris • 23cm

One of the so-called 'dryland kingfishers', this bird forages and nests away from water, often appearing in suburban gardens in coastal areas, from Cape Town to Harare, throughout the bushveld and into the northern suburbs of Johannesburg. Usually seen singly, perched low down at the edge of a clearing or lawn, dropping occasionally to capture insects and other prey. In hot weather, this kingfisher frequently splash-bathes in swimming pools or ponds. Males differ from females in having a black, not brown, back.

Feeding: Takes large insects such as grasshoppers, mantids and beetles, as well as spiders, scorpions, frogs, geckos, skinks and small snakes. Very occasionally takes tadpoles and fishes.

Breeding: Pairs are faithful to one another and occupy a territory year-round. Both sexes help to excavate a nesting tunnel of about 1m into an earthen bank, road cutting or retaining wall. A clutch of four eggs is laid in a chamber at the end, and incubated by the female. Both parents feed the nestlings until they fledge at about 20 days. As with other kingfishers, the nestlings defecate inside the nest, so it smells foul, which may help to deter predators.

Voice: The 'tji! – tu-tu-tu-tu' call is a loud, whistled sequence of four descending notes, with the first note being loudest. Gives a noisy alarm call when startled from its perch.

Lifespan: No data; probably about 12 years.

Garden needs: Open areas bordered by trees from which to perch and hunt. May nest in an earthen embankment or loose stone wall.

Similar species: The Woodland Kingfisher is a summer visitor to the northern and eastern parts of southern Africa where it can be seen in parks, golf courses and large gardens as far south as Gauteng.

This juvenile Brown-hooded Kingfisher (left) is coated in dirt, having just emerged from its nesting burrow in an earth bank.

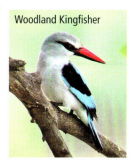

Woodland Kingfisher

RED-FACED MOUSEBIRD

Urocolius indicus • **32cm**

With its scarlet facial mask, this is the most eye-catching of the three southern African mousebirds, aptly named for their grey plumage, long tails and habit of clambering around in bushes. They are never seen singly, but rather in family groups of up to nine, often observed in rapid flight, calling as they go. The Red-faced Mousebird is usually shyer than the Speckled, rarely allowing a close approach. The sexes are alike and the juvenile has a yellow facial mask.

Cape Ash *Ekebergia capensis* is just one of many fruiting plants that attract the Red-faced Mousebird. In good light, the plumage is distinctly bluish-grey.

Feeding: Exclusively vegetarian, feeding on berries and larger fruits in orchards or gardens. *Chrysanthemoides*, *Searsia*, *Ficus*, *Ekebergia* and *Tapinanthus* are favoured fruit plants. Will take the berries of alien *Pyracantha*, *Morus* and *Melia*, among others. May raid orchards for apples, grapes and peaches. Also eats flowers, buds and leaves, as well as aloe nectar.

Breeding: Courtship between a pair includes a bouncing display followed by allopreening prior to mating. The pair is usually assisted by at least one helper throughout the breeding cycle. A flimsy cup-shaped nest, lined with soft material such as plant down or wool, is placed in a tree with thorns or dense foliage. The clutch of 2–3 eggs is incubated for 13 days, and the young fledge at between 14 and 20 days, often leaving the nest earlier if disturbed.

Voice: A musical, three-noted whistle, usually given in flight – 'szii-szii-szii' – not unlike that of the White-faced Whistling Duck.

Lifespan: Eight years recorded, but a captive bird reached 12 years.

Garden needs: Berry-bearing bushes attract these mousebirds. Will also visit feeding tables with soft fruit, and drinks regularly. Enjoys dust bathing in patches of dry sand.

Similar species: The Speckled and White-backed mousebirds (opposite) often occur alongside the Red-faced.

SPECKLED MOUSEBIRD
Colius striatus • **33cm**

With grey plumage, a long tail and the habit of clambering through bushes, mousebirds are aptly named. The Speckled Mousebird is the most familiar species in most South African gardens, although uncommon in Zimbabwe and southern Botswana, and absent from Namibia. In the semi-arid western regions, it is replaced by the White-backed Mousebird. This mousebird is usually seen in small family groups of five or more, moving from place to place in a random, unhurried manner. Sexes are alike; the juvenile has a pale yellow bill.

Feeding: Exclusively vegetarian, feeding on berries and larger fruits in orchards or gardens. *Chrysanthemoides*, *Searsia*, *Ficus*, *Ekebergia* and *Tapinanthus* are favoured. Takes the berries of alien *Pyracantha*, *Morus* and *Melia*, among others, and may raid orchards for apples, grapes and peaches.

Breeding: Family groups occupy a small territory around their nest site. The mated pair is often assisted by up to six helpers, including some unrelated birds. A bowl-shaped nest of fine twigs is lined with soft material (sometimes hair or wool) and concealed within a dense or thorny shrub. Three eggs are incubated. Nestlings fledge after about 17 days but often leave the nest earlier.

Voice: Sharp chattering to maintain contact in the flock. Calls loudly when disturbed.

Lifespan: Eight years recorded.

Garden needs: Berry-bearing bushes, and feeding tables with soft fruit. Drinks regularly. Enjoys dust bathing in patches of dry sand.

Similar species: The White-backed Mousebird is a common garden visitor in the drier western half of the region, ranging as far east as Gauteng.

This mousebird feeds mainly on fruit and berries, but also takes flowers, buds and leaves, as well as aloe nectar.

White-backed Mousebird

WHITE-RUMPED SWIFT
Apus caffer • **16cm**

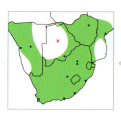

Swifts are remarkable birds, able to spend long periods in flight, riding the air currents without a wingbeat. Many people confuse swifts with swallows, but swallows have broad wings, which allow for balletic flight, and they frequently perch on wires and branches. Swifts, by contrast, slice through the air with their narrow, rigid, sickle-shaped wings, and their tiny feet do not allow them to perch on wires or tree branches. The deeply forked tail is a distinguishing feature of the White-rumped Swift, a summer migrant throughout the region. Usually seen in pairs or family groups, but large numbers may gather to feed in flocks. Sexes alike.

Feeding: An aerial feeder that scoops small winged insects out of the air, usually feeding in the company of other swifts and swallows. May swoop so low as to almost touch the ground. Most active at dusk and after rain.

Breeding: Pairs typically usurp the newly built mud nests of swallows, constructed under veranda ceilings, carports or bridges. The swift pair will line the nest with feathers, which protrude from the tunnel, making it immediately obvious who the occupants are. (Swallows line their egg chamber with feathers but *never* the tunnel.) Both sexes incubate the clutch of two eggs for 22 days, and the young fledge at about 40 days – a lengthy period for such a small bird.

Voice: Trills and buzzing notes are given around the nest, with high-pitched screeching when groups display in flight.

Lifespan: Ten years recorded.

Garden needs: Feeds high above the garden, but will scoop up swimming-pool water in flight. Swifts will be attracted to gardens where swallows are breeding. Most people prefer the swallows, since they put the work into building a nest, but swifts are fascinating to observe at close quarters.

Similar species: The Little Swift is common in towns across the region. It is distinguished by its short, square tail, and flies around urban areas in tight flocks.

This hand-held White-rumped Swift (**left**) shows the deep eye orbits and feathered eyelids typical of the family.

Little Swift

AFRICAN PALM SWIFT
Cypsiurus parvus • **15cm**

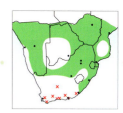

This dashing boomerang-shaped swift flies at terrific speed. It is uniform pale brown and lacks the charcoal-and-white rump typical of swifts in the genus *Apus*. As its name suggests, it is associated with palm trees, and its range has expanded thanks to the cultivation of ornamental *Washingtonia* palms in towns and on farms. Usually seen in small flocks of 5–10, but larger numbers may gather, especially ahead of thunderstorms. Sexes alike.

Feeding: An aerial insectivore usually feeding just above the treetops. Winged ants, fig wasps, termites, bugs and beetles have been recorded in its diet.

Breeding: Pairs or colonies occupy palm trees with large fan-shaped leaves, most often ornamental *Washingtonia*, but traditionally tall *Hyphaene* and *Borassus* palms. The birds use their saliva to attach a small nest of feathers to the underside of a dry, downward-hanging palm leaf, and two eggs are glued to this remarkable structure in the same way. Both parents help to incubate the eggs for 20 days, and the chicks fledge at about 30 days.

Voice: Gives a high-pitched screech in flight.

Lifespan: Three years recorded, but probably lives to at least eight years.

Garden needs: A mature *Washingtonia* palm with a full 'skirt' of dry leaves may attract these fascinating birds. They also skim pools and large ponds to drink.

Small groups of African Palm Swifts swoop and glide around the palm trees in which they roost and nest, sometimes joining other swifts and swallows to feed on small airborne insects.

Similar species: The larger Bradfield's Swift is common around Windhoek and arid regions southwards to Upington and Kimberley.

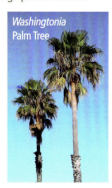

Washingtonia Palm Tree

GREATER STRIPED SWALLOW
Cecropis cucullata • 19cm

One of two similar blue-backed swallows with striped underparts, this is the more widespread, occurring from the southern Cape, through the Karoo and onto the high plateau of Namibia and Zimbabwe. The Greater Striped Swallow has learned to coexist with humans, making use of open verandas and other sheltered spots as nesting sites. Typically occurs in pairs or small family groups, arriving in August and departing by mid-May. The sexes are alike. Distinguished from the Lesser Striped Swallow by its finely streaked underparts and white ear coverts.

Feeding: An aerial feeder; it soars low over open areas, feeding on winged insects such as flies, ants, termites and bugs, often in the company of other swallows and swifts.

Breeding: The pair use mud pellets to build a bowl-shaped nest with a long entrance tunnel, which is stuck in the corner of a veranda, open garage or some such sheltered structure. In the absence of man-made structures, the nest is built on a rock overhang or the underside of a large tree branch. Mud is gathered from rain puddles or the muddy fringe of a pond or dam. The nest usually takes about two weeks to complete, but the builders are frequently dispossessed by White-rumped Swifts and must then begin again. A clutch of three eggs is laid on a bed of dry grass and feathers and incubated for about 18 days by the female only, but the male spends the night in the nest too. Nestlings are fed by both parents and fledge at about 26 days.

Voice: Gives a series of churring nasal notes.

Lifespan: Six years recorded.

Garden needs: Feeds over open areas and is attracted to open-sided buildings in which to nest.

Similar species: The Lesser Striped Swallow (opposite) may occur alongside the Greater in gardens in Gauteng, East London and Port Elizabeth.

Swallows of all species gather feathers to line their nests; one of these Greater Striped Swallows **(above left)** has found a guineafowl feather.

LESSER STRIPED SWALLOW
Cecropis abyssinica • **17cm**

 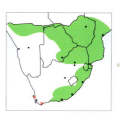

Similar in appearance to the Greater Striped Swallow, but more slimly built and brightly coloured. Sexes are alike. This is the species that favours warmer bushveld and coastal regions, but it has expanded its range in recent decades and may occur alongside the Greater Striped Swallow in Gauteng and other parts of the South African highveld.

Feeding: Feeds aerially on winged insects, including flies, ants, termites and bugs. It soars low down over open areas and is often accompanied by other swallows and swifts.

Breeding: Over a period of about two weeks, members of a pair build a bowl-shaped mud-pellet nest, stuck to the ceiling of a veranda, open garage or similarly sheltered structure. In the absence of man-made structures, the nest is built on a rock overhang or the underside of a large tree branch. They use mud from rain puddles or taken from the margins of ponds or dams. The builders are frequently dispossessed by White-rumped Swifts and must begin again. The female lays a clutch of three eggs and incubates them for about 20 days, and the male joins her in the nest at night. Both parents feed the nestlings, which fledge at about 19 days.

Voice: Gives a series of slow, descending, nasal whistles: 'zeee-zeee-szee-ze-ze'.

Lifespan: Five years recorded.

Garden needs: Feeds over open areas and is attracted to open-sided buildings in which to nest.

Similar species: The Greater Striped Swallow (opposite) may occur alongside the Lesser in gardens in Gauteng, East London and Port Elizabeth.

Lesser Striped Swallows are invariably seen in pairs, usually close to their mud-cup nesting site.

BARN SWALLOW
Hirundo rustica • **20cm**

This is the swallow that most people think of when they consider the passing of the seasons. Millions arrive in southern Africa from Europe each year, some in September but most in late October and November, before returning north again by April. They come here to escape the cold northern winter and to take advantage of the annual proliferation of minute winged insects that occurs during summer. Large flocks gather on overhead wires and roost in reedbeds at dusk. The sexes are alike.

Feeding: Small winged insects are scooped up in flight with an open gape. Always in flocks, often in the company of other swallows and swifts, which they usually outnumber. Most active in the late afternoon. Barn Swallows frequently forage around cattle and other livestock where flies abound and, in coastal areas, they sweep along the surfline to snap up kelp flies and beachhoppers.

Breeding: Breeds in Eurasia.

Voice: The call is a high-pitched twitter.

Lifespan: Seventeen years recorded.

Garden needs: Will perch on overhead wires, roofs and fences in the suburbs and hawk small flying insects around fig trees and compost heaps. In coastal areas, flowering White Milkwoods *Sideroxylon inerme* are visited by swarms of small pollinating flies, which attract Barn Swallows.

Note: Ringing studies show that many of the swallows that spend summer in southern Africa come from Britain. The journey of over 10,000km takes about six weeks, with the swallows moving an average of about 300km per day, feeding as they go.

Similar species: The White-throated Swallow may visit gardens close to sizeable waterbodies in Cape Town, Durban and Gauteng.

Towards the end of summer, Barn Swallows form large flocks that line up along overhead wires and fences, in preparation for their 10,000km return journey north.

ROCK MARTIN

Hirundo fuligula • **12cm**

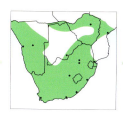

Martins can be thought of as swallows that lack tail streamers, although this definition is not foolproof, since some swallows, such as the South African Cliff Swallow, have square tails. The sandy-brown Rock Martin is a bird of cliffs and rocky outcrops, but has taken to man-made structures. These birds show little fear of people and regularly roost and nest under eaves and verandas. They are resident over most of southern Africa and are usually seen in small family groups. The sexes are alike and the young are distinguished only by their fleshy gape.

Feeding: An aerial feeder, hawking flies and other winged insects. Often in the company of other swallows and swifts, but usually forages close to the ground or, in mountainous areas, alongside cliffs. In coastal areas, it regularly hawks above the intertidal zone.

Breeding: Pairs build an open half-cup nest of mud pellets, with no entrance tunnel, under a rocky ledge or in the top corner of a veranda just below the ceiling. Both parents build the nest, which is usually completed within 20 days. Two broods may be raised in a single season, and the nest is often repaired and reused in successive years. A clutch of 2–3 eggs is incubated for 20 days by both sexes, and the young fledge after 26 days. The young may roost in the nest for up to three weeks.

Voice: A soft twittering call.

Lifespan: Seven years recorded.

Garden needs: Open areas in which to forage, and suitably sheltered sites for nest-building and roosting.

Similar species: The smaller Brown-throated Martin may hawk insects above ponds and dams on larger estates or golf courses in Gauteng, Cape Town and other parts of the region.

Rock Martins huddle together to roost on windowsills, ledges and even outdoor light fittings at night. The juvenile (**above right**) has a conspicuous yellow gape.

FORK-TAILED DRONGO

Dicrurus adsimilis • 25cm

With its jet-black plumage and long, forked tail, the drongo is well known for its habit of attacking and chasing off the largest of raptors – it's the cloak-wearing superhero of the bird world! Perches prominently, often in pairs. Its range has expanded with the spread of Australian *Eucalyptus* trees, and it frequently visits suburban gardens where it can become quite tame and approachable. The sexes are alike, and the juvenile has scaly, dark grey plumage.

Feeding: Launches itself from a perch to capture bees, wasps, termites, butterflies, grasshoppers and beetles. Often follows larger animals, including humans, because they disturb prey as they walk. Quick to attend bush and grass fires to seize fleeing insects. May be active well after dark, feeding on moths around outdoor lights. Also feeds on the nectar of *Aloe* and *Agave* species.

Breeding: Pairs defend a territory throughout the year, building a beautiful shallow cup nest out of rootlets and plant stems bound with cobwebs and located in the outer fork of a horizontal branch. Both sexes build the nest, completing the job in less than a week. A clutch of three eggs is incubated for 16 days by both parents, with the young fledging at about 18 days.

Voice: A range of metallic twanging notes form a jumbled song, but the drongo is also able to mimic the calls of other birds, including that of the Pearl-spotted Owlet.

Lifespan: Six years recorded, but likely to reach at least 10 years.

Garden needs: Requires taller trees on the edges of lawns or other open areas. Uses fences, walls and roofs for perching. May visit bird tables if mealworms are provided.

Similar species: The Square-tailed Drongo is a forest bird, but may occur in gardens in far northern KwaZulu-Natal.

At close quarters, the crimson-red eyes of the drongo are distinctive, but the fishtail-shaped tail is its standout feature.

SOUTHERN BLACK FLYCATCHER
Melaenornis pammelaina • **19cm**

 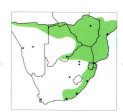

Sometimes forages alongside, and may be confused with, the Fork-tailed Drongo, but this is a slimmer bird, with squared-off tail feathers. Interestingly, the similarity in their plumage may be a form of mimicry that gives an advantage to the flycatcher, since many smaller birds and even raptors give way to the pugnacious drongo. Occurs in the warmer bushveld regions, the lowveld and KwaZulu-Natal, and as far south as Port Elizabeth. Usually seen singly or in pairs, perched on the low outer branches of a tree or on a washing line or fence. The sexes are alike.

Feeding: An insectivore that captures most of its prey by dropping to the ground from its perch or snatching invertebrates from leaves and bark. Hawks winged insects from the air less often than do other flycatchers. Grasshoppers, beetles and spiders are regularly taken. Often joins mixed feeding groups alongside white-eyes, batises and woodpeckers.

Breeding: Pairs occupy a territory throughout the year, but no courtship behaviour has been documented. Constructs a bowl-shaped nest of thin twigs and other plant fibres in a cavity such as a natural tree hole or among the dry fronds of a tree aloe or palm. Also nests in man-made structures such as eaves, pump houses or old machinery.

Voice: The song is a series of clear whistled notes, 'tseep-tsoo-tsoo', as well as other soft vocalisations.

Lifespan: Eight years recorded.

Garden needs: Small trees, with open areas in which to hunt; areas with leaf litter will host more prey than lawns do. Will visit bird tables if mealworms are provided, and may use a birdbath in hot weather.

Similar species: Often confused with the Fork-tailed Drongo (see main text above) or even the male Black Cuckooshrike, both of which are unrelated.

This flycatcher typically forages low down, often clinging to vertical tree trunks from which it sallies out after insect prey.

SPOTTED FLYCATCHER

Muscicapa striata • 14cm

This bird has a misleading name, because no part of its body can be considered spotted! The crown is noticeably streaked, which, together with some of its habits, helps to distinguish it from the similar flycatchers with which it shares its range in southern Africa. The sexes are alike. Typically, it sallies out in pursuit of winged insects and then, upon landing, flicks its wings rapidly, just once. Spotted Flycatchers arrive from Europe in October, often taking up their seasonal residence in the very same patch of bush, farmland or suburbia each year. In early April they return to Europe to breed.

Feeding: Largely insectivorous, capturing insects such as flies, moths, bugs, damselflies and winged ants by launching itself from a fence or some other low perch. Venomous bees and wasps are knocked against a branch to dislodge the stinger prior to being swallowed. Like other flycatchers, it has long rictal bristles projecting from the base of the bill, which assist it in capturing its prey. Occasionally it may feed on the small berries of trees such as *Trema* and *Ochna*.

Breeding: Does not breed in Africa.

Voice: Usually silent when not breeding.

Lifespan: Eleven years recorded.

Garden needs: Lawns and open areas fringed by low-branching trees. An active compost heap may attract this flycatcher.

Similar species: The African Dusky Flycatcher (featured opposite) may occur alongside the Spotted in coastal gardens, but prefers shady habitats.

As its name suggests, the Spotted Flycatcher – like other members of the family – feeds primarily on flies, but any winged insect will be snapped up.

An English garden like this one, which falls within the Spotted Flycatcher's European breeding range, may provide suitable nesting opportunities.

AFRICAN DUSKY FLYCATCHER
Muscicapa adusta • 13cm

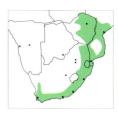

This small forest-dwelling flycatcher enters well-wooded gardens, often becoming very tame and perching on washing lines and fences. Occurs in damp wooded regions from the Cape Peninsula to KwaZulu-Natal, in the escarpment forests of Mpumalanga and Limpopo, and into Zimbabwe. Usually seen singly, it forages in shady areas. Males and females are alike, and the juvenile has buff-spotted upperparts. Distinguished from the similar Spotted Flycatcher by its plain crown and shorter wings, and from the Ashy Flycatcher by its brown rather than grey plumage.

Feeding: Entirely insectivorous, launching out from its perch to hawk for flies, midges, mosquitoes and other winged insects with a sharp snap of the bill. Like other flycatchers, it has long rictal bristles that assist in capturing its prey. Very occasionally it eats berries such as those of *Trema*, *Antidesma*, *Vepris* and alien *Morus*.

Breeding: A bulky open cup nest is placed in a cavity of some kind, typically a hole in the trunk of an old tree or a crevice in a shaded earth bank, but it sometimes nests on a ledge, in a wall cavity or in a hanging plant holder. The nest is roughly built from stems and leaves and is lined with feathers. The female incubates a clutch of three eggs for 15 days, and the young fledge at around 17 days.

Voice: The song is a series of soft whistles, falling in pitch, often given throughout the day. Also gives a variety of scolding alarm notes.

Lifespan: Just three years recorded, but the closely related Spotted Flycatcher has been known to live for 11 years.

Garden needs: Large trees that provide reliable shade. An active compost heap may attract flies and, in turn, flycatchers. May visit a bird table if mealworms are provided, and often comes to birdbaths.

Similar species: the Spotted Flycatcher (opposite) may occur alongside the Dusky in coastal gardens, but prefers more open, sunny habitats and is a migrant present only from October to April.

The African Dusky Flycatcher finds well-wooded gardens much to its liking. It often hawks insect prey from washing lines.

ASHY FLYCATCHER
Muscicapa caerulescens • **14cm**

 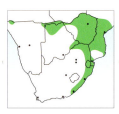

Similar in appearance to the African Dusky and Spotted flycatchers but is blue-grey overall, hence its former name, the Blue-grey Flycatcher. In southern Africa it is restricted to the warmer lowveld and northeastern coastal regions, entering well-wooded gardens in towns such as Durban, Nelspruit and Harare. The male and female are alike, and the immature has a mottled breast and buff-spotted back. May be seen singly, in pairs or among other insectivorous birds in mixed feeding groups.

Feeding: An insectivore that captures prey by hawking from a perch or gleaning leaves and bark. Flies, midges, bugs and moths are regularly taken, but occasionally takes large mantids and even small tree geckos. Like other flycatchers, it has a compressed bill and long rictal bristles that assist in capturing its prey. Occasionally eats small berries from trees such as *Trema* and *Antidesma*.

Breeding: Pairs occupy a territory throughout the year. They bow their wings and point their bills skywards in courtship display, prior to breeding. A bowl-shaped nest made of bark strips, grass and tendrils is lined with soft lichen or moss (never feathers) and placed in a cavity such as a tree hole or a crevice in a wall. The female incubates a clutch of three eggs for 14 days, and the young fledge after a further 14 days.

Voice: The song is a soft but distinctive 'tsip-tsip-tsip-tseep', heard most often at dawn and dusk.

Lifespan: Three years recorded, but 11 years recorded for the related Spotted Flycatcher.

Garden needs: Well-wooded gardens with widely spaced leafy trees. Drinks and bathes regularly and visits birdbaths.

The juvenile Ashy Flycatcher (**left**) is heavily blotched and spotted to provide camouflage from predators. This is a trait shared by all *Muscicapa* flycatchers.

Similar species: The Marico Flycatcher is a common garden bird in dry bushveld towns such as Windhoek, Gaborone and Bulawayo, south to Pretoria.

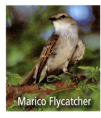

Marico Flycatcher

FISCAL FLYCATCHER

Sigelus silens • 18cm

At first glance, this bird resembles the Southern Fiscal, as it has an almost identical black-and-white colour pattern and shares the habit of perching conspicuously on fences, gateposts and the outer branches of trees. However, on closer inspection, this flycatcher has a much more slender bill and a proportionately smaller head; in flight, the white panels in the tail are conspicuous. More or less endemic to South Africa, but with populations in southern Botswana and Swaziland. Common in the Cape and on the highveld, but a scarce winter migrant to the lowveld and KwaZulu-Natal coast. The female is smoky brown rather than glossy black.

Feeding: Primarily insectivorous, dropping down onto ants, beetles, termites, grasshoppers and other invertebrates from a perch. Less often, it sallies out to catch flies, moths and other insects. Occasionally feeds on small berries such as those of *Halleria*.

Breeding: Pairs occupy a territory throughout the year, performing a tail-fanning and head-bowing courtship display, and sometimes the male presents his mate with a gift of downy plant material. The bulky cup-shaped nest is built out of dry plant stems in the fork of a tree, and is lined with soft seedheads or feathers. The female incubates the clutch of three eggs for 15 days, and the young fledge at around 17 days.

Voice: The male sings with a series of soft, high-pitched whistles and sometimes mimics the calls of other species, including robin-chats, mousebirds and sunbirds.

Lifespan: Nine years recorded.

Garden needs: Open areas with suitable perches and shrubs for nesting. May visit bird tables for mealworms.

Similar species: None, but often confused with the larger Southern Fiscal (see notes above).

The male and female Fiscal Flycatcher are never far apart, frequently perching together. As with other flycatchers, the juvenile (**above right**) is spotted.

AFRICAN PARADISE FLYCATCHER

Terpsiphone viridis • 17cm (♂ up to 37cm with tail streamers)

Swooping between tree branches like a miniature orange rocket, this dazzling bird is one of the most cherished garden visitors. It favours riparian and kloof forest from Cape Town northwards into KwaZulu-Natal, along lowveld rivers, and in the bushveld southwards into Johannesburg. Common throughout Zimbabwe and eastern and northern Botswana. The male sports long, streamer-like tail feathers and has a brighter blue bill and broader eye wattles than the female. Usually seen in pairs, energetically hawking flies and other insects in shady well-wooded areas.

The male African Paradise Flycatcher has long, ribbon-like tail feathers and broad eye wattles. The female is duller than the male, with a shorter tail.

Feeding: Captures prey in flight after a jinking pursuit. Typically hunts from within a shady tree and often alongside other birds in mixed feeding groups, or in association with large mammals that serve as beaters. Butterflies, moths, damselflies, fruit flies and mosquitoes are common prey; often skims drowned insects from swimming pools.

Breeding: Throughout much of southern Africa this is a summer visitor. Males usually arrive before females and defend territories into which they attract a mate. The tiny egg-cup nest is built of thin strips of plant material and bound into a narrow tree fork with cobwebs, often in a fairly exposed position. The nest is camouflaged with blue and grey lichen. For 15 days the parents incubate the clutch of three eggs in alternating half-hour shifts. The young fledge at 15 days old.

Voice: Vociferous, especially in the period leading up to laying. The male gives a liquid whistled song, like ripples of tiny laughter. Also gives a 'chweet-cwheet' alarm or contact call. Quick to mob snakes, owls and goshawks as well as nest-robbing bush-shrikes and monkeys.

Lifespan: Eleven years recorded.

Garden needs: Shady areas, a pond or pool in which to splash-bathe, and fruit-bearing trees to attract its fruit fly prey.

Similar species: None. The related Blue-mantled Crested Flycatcher, which has a very similar voice, may visit well-wooded coastal gardens.

CAPE BATIS

Batis capensis • **12cm**

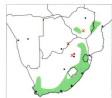

This small black-and-white bird has a relatively large head and typically adopts a hunched posture, appearing almost ball-shaped. The Cape Batis is often inquisitive towards people and may draw attention to itself with its rasping alarm call or clear three-noted 'whu-whu-whu' whistle. Occurs at the edges of forests and thickets from the southern Cape to KwaZulu-Natal and at high elevations in Mpumalanga, often entering gardens in these regions. Male and female are quite different in appearance and are usually seen together.

Feeding: Insectivorous, moving restlessly through trees snatching spiders, bugs, beetles, ants and other insects with an audible bill snap. Often forages low down and joins mixed feeding groups, including woodpeckers, to glean insects disturbed by the moving flock.

Breeding: Pairs occupy a territory throughout the year. The tiny cup-shaped nest is fashioned from thin plant stems and rootlets, bound to a narrow fork in a small tree using cobwebs. The outside is decorated with grey lichen that often matches the surrounding branches and provides camouflage. The female incubates the clutch of two eggs for 18 days, and the young leave the nest after a further 16 days. May be parasitised by the Klaas's Cuckoo.

Voice: Both male and female give a loud three-noted whistle – 'whu-whu-whu'. Also give a rasping 'kshee-kshee' alarm call and are among the first birds to take alarm at owls, snakes and other predators.

Lifespan: Eight years recorded.

Garden needs: Shady wooded areas; rarely, if ever, visits a feeding station or birdbath.

Similar species: The Chinspot Batis may visit gardens adjacent to bushveld in towns such as Pretoria, Gaborone and Bulawayo.

Chinspot Batis

The male Cape Batis has a broad black chest bar and white throat, while the female is more muted in appearance. Their courtship display includes zigzag flights with bill-snapping and fanned-out tails.

KAROO PRINIA
Prinia maculosa • **14 cm**

A tiny bird with a big personality, this prinia is restricted to the fynbos, strandveld and Karoo regions of the Cape. Usually seen singly or in pairs, calling loudly from the top of a bush with its tail raised. Quick to appear when a snake, cat or other predator is about, calling out in alarm to drive the threat away. At such times, bulbuls, apalises and other birds often join it. Male and female are alike, and the immature is barely distinguishable.

Feeding: An arboreal insectivore that plucks caterpillars, ants, bugs and other insects from leaves and flowers. Always forages low down and frequently hops about on the ground to capture termites and other prey.

Breeding: Pairs defend a territory and build an oval nest in a dense shrub. Strips of fresh green grass are woven together, fading as they age and dry out. The inside is lined with the soft fluffy seedheads of *Eriocephalus* and *Tarchonanthus*. The female incubates a clutch of four eggs for about 14 days, and the young fledge about 14 days after hatching. Nests are occasionally parasitised by Diederik and Klaas' cuckoos.

Voice: Gives a strident 'kli-kli-kli-kli' call and a rasping 'krrrt-krrrt'.

Lifespan: Five years recorded.

Garden needs: Indigenous plants such as *Searsia* and *Salvia* will host suitable invertebrate prey and also provide nesting sites. May be tempted onto bird tables with mealworms.

Similar species: The Tawny-flanked Prinia may visit garden thickets in the warmer eastern parts of the region, while the Black-chested Prinia is common in parts of Gauteng and westwards to Windhoek.

This species usually only visits gardens adjacent to natural vegetation, but it is noisy, bold and unafraid of people.

Tawny-flanked Prinia

BAR-THROATED APALIS
Apalis thoracica • **12 cm**

This tiny, long-tailed bird occurs throughout most of southern Africa, except for the semi-arid Karoo and Kalahari regions, and through most of Zimbabwe too. Thirteen distinct races exist; those in the southwestern Cape have a grey back and off-white underparts, while those in the foothills of the escarpment in Mpumalanga are markedly different, with an olive-green back and yellow underparts. Although small, this apalis is restless and very vocal, so it is a familiar garden bird in suburbs close to forests, thickets or dune scrub. Male and female are alike.

A. t. spelonkensis

A. t. thoracica

In the southern Cape, this apalis is predominantly grey and cream **(top)**, whereas populations in the north and east are olive and pale yellow **(above)**.

Feeding: An insectivore, it picks small insects from foliage, flowers and bark – ants, weevils, bugs, caterpillars and spiders feature in its diet.

Breeding: Pairs establish a territory and proclaim their occupancy with frequent bouts of calling. The nest is a small oval ball made of thin plant stems such as *Asparagus*, as well as moss and lichen, often lined with soft downy material such as the seedheads of *Eriocephalus* and *Tarchonanthus*. The structure is hidden within foliage, attached to a small sapling or creeper. Both sexes incubate the clutch of three eggs for 15 days, and the young fledge 15 days later.

Voice: Gives a repetitive 'tlip-tlip-tlip-tlip-tlip', from within cover or from the top of a bush. Also various harsh alarm notes. Quick to mob snakes, cats and mongooses.

Lifespan: Nine years recorded.

Garden needs: Favours dense shrubberies and thickets. A hedge or thicket of *Searsia* or some other evergreen shrub will attract this species, as long as your garden is alongside, or close to, natural vegetation.

Similar species: The Yellow-breasted Apalis visits well-wooded gardens in towns such as Durban, Nelspruit, Hoedspruit and Maun.

Yellow-breasted Apalis

WILLOW WARBLER
Phylloscopus trochilus • **12cm**

This tiny bird is a migrant from Eurasia and one of the easiest to overlook in any garden. It occurs across the whole region but is more or less silent, lacks bright coloration and keeps mostly to the leafy canopies of taller trees. The sexes appear the same – pale greenish-grey above, with a thin yellow supercilium and a dark eye stripe; the underparts are tinged yellow. The closely related and similar-looking Icterine and Garden warblers are also non-breeding summer migrants from Eurasia.

Feeding: Plucks aphids and other small insects from leaves, twigs and flowers in the canopy of large shrubs and trees. Completely arboreal and rarely gets close to the ground.

Breeding: This little bird breeds in Europe, where it often nests in stands of willow trees along the edges of bogs and marshes, or in oak or birch woods.

Voice: In Africa, it is mostly silent, but it does give an occasional soft, musical, warbled song, presumably as practice, prior to undertaking its 10,000km-long migration back to Europe.

Lifespan: Two years recorded, but probably reaches at least five years.

Garden needs: Tall trees, particularly acacias, as they harbour plenty of small invertebrates.

Similar species: There are numerous confusingly similar species of small warbler, most of which are also non-breeding visitors from Eurasia. The Garden Warbler is an uncommon, easily overlooked example. The Green-backed Camaroptera is a resident African warbler, common in well-wooded gardens from Port Elizabeth to Nelspruit.

The Willow Warbler forages quietly in tree canopies, pulling caterpillars, like this Common Bush Brown, from leaves and snapping up bugs, spiders and any other small invertebrates it finds.

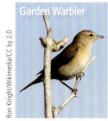
Garden Warbler

Green-backed Camaroptera

BLACK-HEADED ORIOLE
Oriolus larvatus • **25 cm**

With its bright lemon-yellow underparts and rosy-pink bill protruding from its coal black head, this is a strikingly beautiful bird. It is restricted to the warmer well-wooded eastern and northern parts of South Africa, but sometimes ventures into parts of Johannesburg where the suburbs are now extensively wooded. Calls from a high perch but forages within leafy canopies, so it can go undetected if its voice is not known. Occurs singly or in pairs. The sexes are alike. Juveniles are streaky, with a dark brown bill.

Feeding: Largely insectivorous, this oriole captures most of its prey by inspecting the undersides of leaves for caterpillars, bugs, mantids and katydids. Also feeds on the nectar of *Aloe*, *Schotia* and *Erythrina*, as well as that of alien trees such as *Acrocarpus*, *Grevillea* and *Eucalyptus*.

Breeding: Pairs occupy a territory throughout the year. They display with fanned tails and quivering wings prior to mating. A hammock-like cup nest of dry grass and plant fibres is slung between twigs on a horizontal stem of an outer tree branch, and attached with cobweb. A clutch of three eggs is incubated by both sexes for about 15 days, and the young leave the nest about 17 days after hatching.

Voice: The most common call is a loud, liquid 'kleeeuw!' repeated at intervals, but it also gives a variety of strange grating calls and is able to mimic the voices of other birds.

Lifespan: No data; probably reaches at least eight years.

Garden needs: Needs tall, leafy trees in which to forage and nest. Will visit stands of flowering aloes.

Similar species: The Eurasian Golden Oriole is an uncommon, non-breeding summer migrant that can appear in gardens throughout the region; it has an entirely yellow head.

The Black-headed Oriole often calls from the very top of a tree canopy, where it can be difficult to see.

Tim Cockcroft

AFRICAN RED-EYED BULBUL

Pycnonotus nigricans • 20 cm

This is the dry-country counterpart of the Dark-capped and Cape bulbuls. It occurs throughout the Karoo and Kalahari, where it is a common garden bird in towns such as Bloemfontein, Kimberley and Graaff-Reinet. Like its close relatives, it is one of the most conspicuous garden birds and is quick to raise the alarm at the presence of cats, mongooses, owls and snakes. Sexes are alike. Juveniles lack the red eye wattles.

Feeding: Eats fruit and insects in equal quantities and relishes *Aloe* nectar. Favours the berries of *Searsia* and *Boscia*, as well as those of the alien Brazilian Pepper Tree *Schinus molle*. This bulbul is an important seed disperser. Visits orchards to feed on ripe peaches and apricots. Small beetles, caterpillars and spiders are among the invertebrates taken from foliage. Often sallies out to capture winged insects, and comes to the ground more often than the Cape or Dark-capped bulbuls.

Breeding: Pairs defend a territory in which the female builds an open bowl nest of thin plant stems and grass seedheads, concealed within a leafy shrub or tree. The clutch of three eggs is incubated for 12 days by the female, with chicks fledging after 12 days. Nests may be parasitised by the Jacobin Cuckoo.

Voice: The male calls from an exposed perch, giving loud, musical 'tillop-peep-peep-tiddlypop' phrases.

Lifespan: Probably at least eight years.

Like other bulbuls, the African Red-eyed drinks and bathes regularly, so it is a common visitor to gardens within its range.

Garden needs: Berry-producing shrubs and acacias that harbour insects will attract this bulbul. Also visits bird tables for fruit. Drinks and bathes throughout the day, so will be a regular at a birdbath.

Similar species: There is little overlap in the distribution ranges of the three common bulbuls, but the Red-eyed may occur alongside Dark-capped in gardens in southern Gauteng, Gaborone and Maun.

CAPE BULBUL

Pycnonotus capensis • **20cm**

This lively bird is the fynbos and strandveld counterpart of the Dark-capped and African Red-eyed bulbuls. It is a very familiar garden bird in Cape Town, Stellenbosch and other parts of the southern Cape, and occurs as far west as Port Elizabeth. Bulbuls adapt quickly to human-modified landscapes. The Cape Bulbul occurs in pairs or small flocks at abundant food sources. Sexes are alike; juveniles lack the fleshy white eye rings. Endemic to South Africa, where it is confined to the winter-rainfall region.

Feeding: Takes equal amounts of fruit and insects and enjoys the nectar of *Aloe* and *Salvia*. The berries of *Searsia*, *Kiggelaria* and *Chrysanthemoides* are particularly favoured, and these bulbuls are important seed dispersers for coastal shrubs and trees. Takes small beetles, caterpillars, spiders and other invertebrates from foliage.

Breeding: Pairs occupy a small territory, building an open cup nest of grass stems and rootlets, well hidden in the fork of an outer branch. The female builds the nest alone, while her mate keeps watch and sings nearby. The female incubates a clutch of three eggs for 12 days, and the young fledge when they are about 13 days old.

Voice: The loud, warbling song is given from an exposed perch and consists of various repeated 'chip-chee-woodly, chup-wheet-churry-up' phrases. Among the first birds to mob a snake or owl, it gives a deep 'churr' in alarm.

Lifespan: Eight years recorded.

Garden needs: *Chrysanthemoides*, *Searsia*, *Carissa* and other berry-bearing shrubs and trees. Also visits bird tables for fruit, fatty scraps and bonemeal. A regular visitor to birdbaths to drink and bathe.

Similar species: There is little overlap in the distribution ranges of the three common bulbuls, but the Cape may occur alongside the Red-eyed in gardens in the Little Karoo.

The Cape Bulbul is one of the most common and familiar garden birds throughout the winter-rainfall region of South Africa.

DARK-CAPPED BULBUL

Pycnonotus tricolor • **20cm**

Chirpy and bold, this is one of the most conspicuous small birds in the eastern and northern parts of southern Africa, where it is also a very common garden bird. Usually seen in pairs or family groups. The sexes are alike, and the juvenile is little different. Quick to scold cats, mongooses, owls and snakes with a tireless alarm call, often attracting other species to join in and drive the unwelcome predator away.

Feeding: Eats fruit and insects in equal amounts, and relishes the nectar of *Aloe* and *Schotia*. Favours the berries of *Antidesma* and *Trema*, among others, as well as those of invasive *Lantana* and *Solanum*, which it spreads via seed dispersal. Small beetles, caterpillars and spiders are among the invertebrates taken from foliage. Often sallies out to capture winged insects.

Breeding: Pairs occupy a small territory, but numbers may gather at abundant food sources. The female builds an open cup nest of plant stems and dry grass seedheads, concealed in a leafy tree or shrub. She incubates a clutch of three eggs for 13 days, and the chicks fledge after another 13 days. Nests may be parasitised by the Jacobin Cuckoo.

Voice: Perches conspicuously, giving a loud warbling song consisting of various repeated phrases – 'chip-chok-tchwik – chip-chok-chip-kweeo'. Gives other contact and alarm calls.

Lifespan: Twelve years recorded, but one captive bird lived to 26!

Garden needs: Attracted to berry-producing shrubs and acacias that harbour insects. Visits bird tables for fruit. Drinks and bathes throughout the day, so will be a regular at birdbaths.

Similar species: The Dark-capped may occur alongside the Red-eyed in gardens in southern Gauteng, Gaborone and Maun.

The actual purpose of the yellow vent is unknown, but it is a feature shared by numerous birds, including the Cape Sugarbird, p.124.

SOMBRE GREENBUL
Andropadus importunus • 22cm

More often heard than seen, this is a secretive but common bird along the coast from Cape Town to Mozambique, as well as in the lowveld and in the Eastern Highlands of Zimbabwe. It is a frequent garden resident or visitor in towns such as Cape Town, Hermanus, Port Elizabeth, Durban and Nelspruit. Usually seen singly or in pairs. It is identified by its startling pale eyes, plain olive-brown plumage and distinctive call. Sexes alike.

A. i. importunus

A. i. mentor

The Sombre Greenbul has no noteworthy plumage features, but its pale creamy-white eyes are distinctive. This bird sings throughout the day, year-round, from the top of a bush or tree. Three races occur in the region, with populations in the Cape being dark olive-brown (**above**), while those in the northeast are brighter yellow-green (**left**).

Feeding: Consumes equal quantities of fruit and invertebrates, taking them from the foliage of the tree canopy. Also feeds on ripe figs and the berries of trees such as *Antidesma*, *Searsia*, *Berchemia*, *Phyllanthus* and *Ekebergia*. In addition, it eats the berries of *Lantana* and *Solanum*, thus dispersing the seeds of these invasive species. Katydids, mantids, beetles, spiders and caterpillars are among its invertebrate prey.

Breeding: Pairs occupy a territory year-round, advertising with frequent, often monotonous, calling. The female builds an open cup nest of dry grass and bark shreds, which is concealed within foliage. She incubates a clutch of two eggs for 13 days, and the youngsters fledge after a further 13 days. May be parasitised by the Jacobin Cuckoo.

Voice: The piercing whistled call sounds like 'Willy! – Where are you? – Come and fight!'

Lifespan: Twelve years recorded.

Garden needs: Tall, dense, berry-producing trees and shrubs. May visit bird tables for fruit, and may use birdbaths in hot weather.

Similar species: The Terrestrial Brownbul occurs in thickets in well-wooded coastal gardens from Mossel Bay to Mozambique, and in parts of the lowveld, Zimbabwe and northern Botswana.

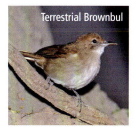

Terrestrial Brownbul

KAROO THRUSH

Turdus smithii • **24cm**

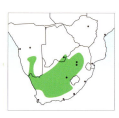

Formerly regarded as a race of the Olive Thrush, this bird occupies the highveld and Karoo, where it can occur in high densities in well-wooded suburban gardens and around homesteads. Differs from the Olive Thrush in being more or less uniformly coloured, lacking buff-orange underparts and in that it has distinctive orange eye rings. The sexes are alike. In recent years, its range has grown considerably due to urban development and the spread of exotic trees.

Feeding: Something of an earthworm specialist, it flicks through leaf litter, tilts its head to listen for movement, and then stabs its bill into soft ground. Earthworms are pulled out and eaten whole. Also feeds on termites, spiders and other ground-living invertebrates, as well as snails, which are bashed against stones or paving to remove their shells. Feeds on fallen fruit and berries such as *Kiggelaria* and *Celtis*, less often picking them directly from trees.

Breeding: Pairs occupy small territories, advertising their presence with dawn and dusk calling. An untidy bowl-shaped nest is made of plant fibres and may include man-made materials such as string. It is built in the fork of a tree, hidden and shaded by foliage. Mud is often added to the rim for strength. The female incubates the clutch of two eggs for 14 days, and chicks fledge at about 16 days. Nests are occasionally parasitised by the Red-chested Cuckoo.

Voice: Gives a warbling, whistled 'wee-it-wee-it, twit-twit, twiddle-it' song, most often at dawn and dusk. Gives a sharp 'tseep' when taking off. Has a harsh churring alarm call and mimics the calls of other birds.

Lifespan: Ten years recorded.

Garden needs: Shade and leaf litter. Will visit bird tables for fruit, cheese and bonemeal. Drinks and bathes throughout the day.

Similar species: Easily confused with the Olive Thrush (featured opposite), but note the difference in distribution.

Thrushes are most active in the low light of dawn and dusk, but will bathe and drink throughout the day.

OLIVE THRUSH

Turdus olivaceus • **24cm**

Until recently, the Olive and Karoo thrushes were regarded as the same species. Many people in Gauteng may be under the impression that the Olive Thrush occurs in their gardens when it is, in fact, the Karoo Thrush that inhabits the highveld and Karoo. The Olive Thrush occupies the higher-rainfall regions of the southern Cape, Garden Route, KwaZulu-Natal coast and Drakensberg escarpment forests. The sexes are alike, with a rich orange belly (much duller in Karoo Thrush) and brown eye rings (orange in Karoo Thrush). The juvenile has spotted underparts.

Feeding: Another earthworm specialist, this thrush also listens for movement as it flicks through leaf litter and stabs its bill into soft ground. Earthworms are eaten whole. Termites, spiders, other ground-living invertebrates and snails are also taken, the snails being smashed to remove their shells first. Picks up fallen fruit and berries and occasionally plucks them straight from trees.

Breeding: In natural forest, pairs are widely separated, but they occur at higher densities in wooded suburbs where food is presumably more abundant. An untidy bowl-shaped nest of plant fibres and, sometimes, man-made materials such as string is hidden in a well-branched, shaded fork of a tree. The rim may be strengthened with mud. A clutch of 2–3 eggs is incubated for 14 days, with chicks fledging at 16 days. May be parasitised by the Red-chested Cuckoo.

Voice: The song is series of clear ringing whistles – 'tweety, wheety, weet' – generally given from a treetop, most often at twilight. Usually calls with a sharp 'tseep' when taking off. Also has a harsh 'chink-chink' alarm call and can mimic the calls of other birds.

Lifespan: Seven years recorded, but likely to exceed 10 years.

Garden needs: Shade and leaf litter. Takes fruit, cheese and bonemeal from bird tables. Drinks and bathes throughout the day.

Similar species: Easily confused with the Karoo Thrush (featured opposite), but note distribution maps.

The juvenile Olive Thrush (**left**) is boldly barred and speckled, providing camouflage that confuses predators.

KURRICHANE THRUSH

Turdus libonyanus • **22cm**

This is the most common thrush of the bushveld and lowveld and is a familiar garden bird in towns across most of KwaZulu-Natal, Mpumalanga and Limpopo; also extends into Zimbabwe and Botswana. It adapts well to human-modified landscapes and is expanding its range south, but rarely occurs alongside the slightly larger Karoo or Olive thrushes. Usually seen singly or in pairs, flipping quietly through leaf litter in the shade of trees. Up to a dozen may gather at food sources in winter. The male and female are alike, and the juvenile is mottled below.

Feeding: Feeds mostly on the ground, searching under leaf litter for earthworms, beetles, ants and spiders as well as small skinks and geckos. Also relishes figs and berries, with *Antidesma*, *Trema* and *Phyllanthus* among its favourites, and feeds on avocados and other fallen fruit in orchards.

Breeding: Pairs occupy territories throughout the year. The female builds a deep bowl-shaped nest in the main fork of a tree – the exterior is rough but finer material is used inside, and wet leaves and mud are often added for strength. Sometimes nests in a hanging plant holder or roof gutter.

Voice: The song is a series of fluty whistles – 'whip-weedle – tyeeoo-weet-weet' – given mostly at dusk and dawn. Usually gives a sharp 'tseep' when taking off. Also has a harsh churring alarm call and can mimic the calls of other birds.

Lifespan: Eight years recorded.

Garden needs: Allowing leaf litter to gather will provide feeding opportunities; also visits bird tables for fruit and fatty foods. Drinks and bathes throughout the day, so is a regular at birdbaths.

Gardens in the northern and eastern parts of southern Africa attract the richly coloured Kurrichane Thrush. It typically runs across open areas, pausing to tilt its head and listen for movement.

Similar species: The Groundscraper Thrush has a similar distribution range but prefers more open habitats such as parks and sports fields.

Groundscraper Thrush

MOCKING CLIFF CHAT
Thamnolaea cinnamomeiventris • 22cm

This bird is often bold around humans, venturing onto porches and verandas in search of food. It is restricted to the eastern half of southern Africa, where it is associated with rocky outcrops and cliffs. However, man-made structures close to these environments offer a similar habitat, and it may take up residence in gardens and around homesteads. The male is a striking combination of glossy charcoal and burnt orange, with white shoulder patches, while the female is a more subdued version and lacks any white. The juvenile has buffy feather tips.

Feeding: Captures beetles, grasshoppers, millipedes, small scorpions and rock-dwelling geckos. Has been seen jumping onto the backs of Klipspringers and Rock Hyrax to take ticks. Also hawks winged termite alates. Occasionally takes figs, the berries of *Commiphora* and other trees, and *Aloe* nectar.

Breeding: Pairs occupy a territory throughout the year, singing from favoured perches to declare occupancy. They select the mud-cup nest of a swallow or martin, usually located under a rock overhang or on the ceiling of a cave, porch or outbuilding. Inside it they construct a shallow bowl of dry plant material and animal hair. May occupy a disused nest or remove the tunnel from an active nest and drive off the resident swallows. Less often, a cavity in a wall or building is used. The female incubates a clutch of three eggs for 14 days, and the young fledge at around 20 days.

Voice: The song is a sequence of clear, fluty whistles, but this bird is a superb mimic, able to imitate the calls of at least 30 bird species, hence the name 'Mocking Cliff Chat'.

Lifespan: No records, but probably attains at least 10 years.

Garden needs: May visit bird tables where mealworms and bonemeal are provided, and regularly inspects dog bowls. Buildings where Greater or Lesser striped swallows or Rock Martins breed may attract this bird.

Similar species: The Cape Rock Thrush may visit gardens close to rocky hillsides, from the southern Cape to Gauteng.

The Mocking Cliff Chat will only appear in gardens if they are adjacent to koppies and other rocky habitats, but it can become very tame, even entering kitchens to take scraps.

FAMILIAR CHAT
Cercomela familiaris • **15cm**

Drab in plumage but lively in personality, this little bird is unafraid of humans and happily forages along pathways, on low walls and at outdoor braai areas. It has the habit of rapidly flicking its wings each time it lands, a useful trait for identification. Usually seen alone or in pairs, searching for invertebrates on the ground or among rocks, or perching prominently on fences, posts and bushes. The male and female are alike. Individuals in the southern Cape are considerably darker than those in the central and eastern regions.

Feeding: Largely insectivorous, snapping up prey after a hopping pursuit, or jumps onto its quarry from a perch. Spiders, millipedes, beetles, ants, termites, crickets, moths, butterflies and larvae are typical prey. Relishes dried meat and fat left on braai grids, as well as pet food. This chat used to eat the animal fat that greased the axles of ox wagons, hence its Afrikaans name *Spekvreter* ('fat eater').

Breeding: Pairs occupy a territory throughout the year. The cup-shaped nest consists of grass stems and other plant material and often string, wool or bits of cloth. It may be supported by soil clumps and stones and is placed in a cavity, very often a man-made structure such as a wall, ledge, pipe or open mailbox. It has been known to enter houses and even to nest in an open cupboard! Three eggs are incubated for 14 days, and the young fledge after a further 14 days.

Voice: Gives series of quiet churring notes. The alarm call is a harsh 'chak-chak'.

Lifespan: Six years recorded.

Garden needs: Will visit bird tables for bonemeal and fatty foods.

Similar species: Although not similar in plumage, the Mountain Wheatear is very closely related to the Familiar Chat and shares many physical and behavioural traits. It may be common in gardens in the Karoo, southern Gauteng and Windhoek.

Few birds are as confiding as the aptly named Familiar Chat, which likes to forage in open areas. It may inspect dog bowls for scraps and use stone walls and outbuildings as nesting sites.

Mountain Wheatear

CAPE WAGTAIL
Motacilla capensis • **20cm**

One of the most widespread and adaptable birds in southern Africa, this wagtail is as happy wandering about lawned suburbs as it is pacing city streets or car parks. Constantly bobbing its long tail, it shows little fear of humans and can often be approached more closely than other birds. Usually seen in pairs, but large numbers gather at communal roosts in winter. Sexes are alike. The juveniles are paler versions of the adults. It is not unusual to see one of these wagtails with missing toes, and although this phenomenon has been blamed on pesticides, it is more likely that small threads from discarded fabrics are to blame: a wagtail's feet can collect these fine fibres and if blood flow to the toes is restricted, they will shrivel up and fall off.

Feeding: An insectivore that captures all manner of small invertebrates, including those in shallow water. A bird of wetland fringes, it has adapted to human-modified landscapes, especially lawns, pastures and sports fields. Frequently takes dead insects killed at outdoor lights and on car grills. In coastal regions it feeds in the intertidal zone.

Breeding: Pairs occupy a small territory in which they build a nest bowl of dry grass and forbs, usually within a wall cavity, hedge or even a flowerpot. It is lined with hair, feathers or soft plant material and is often, but not always, near water. Both sexes incubate the three eggs for 14 days, and the young fledge after about 15 days. Some nests are parasitised by Red-chested Cuckoo.

Voice: A varied jumble of whistled notes, given from an exposed perch.

Lifespan: Eleven years recorded.

Garden needs: Open lawns and wetlands. Seldom visits bird tables or birdbaths.

Similar species: the African Pied Wagtail may visit gardens close to waterbodies from Port Elizabeth northwards into Zimbabwe; also in Upington and towns along the Orange River.

Like others of its kind, the Cape Wagtail is typically a waterside bird but is more often found in man-made habitats, often some distance from streams or dams.

African Pied Wagtail

ARROW-MARKED BABBLER

Turdoides jardinii • 24cm

 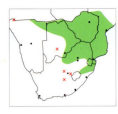

As its name suggests, this is a noisy and restless bird, always seen in chattering family groups of around six members, never alone. A resident in warm bushveld regions where it can be a common garden visitor; in recent years this babbler has become established in the northern parts of Johannesburg. This is one of the first birds to give an alarm call at the sight of a cat, snake or owl. In addition to the arrow-shaped white streaks on the head, mantle and breast, the most distinctive feature is the bright yellow-and-red eyes; the sexes are identical.

Feeding: Largely insectivorous, capturing beetles, mantids, grasshoppers and termites on the ground or on lower branches. Also feeds on the nectar of aloes, and on berries and fruit; will readily visit bird tables where bonemeal or mealworms are provided.

Breeding: This is a cooperative breeder, with all family members assisting in raising the young. A scruffy bowl-shaped nest is made out of plant stems and dry grass, usually placed no higher than 2m in dense foliage or a tangle of brush. Pairs occupy a territory throughout the year, regularly calling to advertise their presence. A clutch of three eggs is incubated by all group members for 13–17 days, and the young leave the nest when they are about 20 days old. Levaillant's Cuckoo occasionally parasitises the nests.

Voice: A series of harsh, nasal notes develops into a chorus of raucous cackling, tailing off in drawn-out slurs 'njaa-njaa-njaa'. All members of the family group vocalise together.

Lifespan: No data, but probably at least eight years.

Garden needs: Thickets are required for cover and nesting. Groups spend much time foraging on the ground, flicking through leaves, but will visit feeding stations and birdbaths.

Similar species: The striking Southern Pied Babbler may visit gardens in dry towns such as Gaborone, Bulawayo and Windhoek.

Arrow-marked Babblers will come regularly to feeding stations where bonemeal is provided; these noisy birds are entertaining to watch.

CAPE ROBIN-CHAT

Cossypha caffra • **17cm**

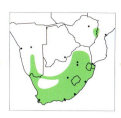

Voted South Africa's favourite bird in a survey by BirdLife South Africa, this is certainly one of the most cherished birds in the country. It is as familiar in Johannesburg as it is in Cape Town. Distinct populations occur in the Eastern Highlands of Zimbabwe as well as in East Africa. Normally seen singly or in pairs, hopping confidently around gardens and porches, getting close to people as they weed or plant, and frequently appearing on bird tables and in birdbaths. The male and female are alike. Youngsters have buffy plumage with a scaly appearance.

Feeding: Largely insectivorous but takes berries from time to time. Moves quickly about on the ground, flicking over leaves to expose beetles, ants, crickets, spiders and other invertebrates. Also takes earthworms from upturned soil.

Breeding: Pairs occupy small territories throughout the year, singing at dawn and dusk to proclaim their ownership. An open cup nest is made out of small twigs, bark strips, grass and leaves, and lined with animal hair or fine rootlets. This is placed in a tree stump cavity, a tangle of creepers, a crevice in a large wall, an open-sided tin or a hanging plant basket. The female incubates a clutch of 2–3 eggs for 16 days, and the young fledge after a further 16 days. Many nests are parasitised by the Red-chested Cuckoo.

Voice: The song is a sequence of soft, clear whistles, most frequently given at dawn and dusk. Sometimes mimics the calls of other birds. The alarm call is a distinctive guttural 'whrrr-durrr', also given when going to roost and to maintain contact with fledglings.

Lifespan: Seventeen years recorded.

Garden needs: Happy in gardens that provide some shady areas and soft soil in which to forage. Leaves decomposing below trees and bushes provide an ideal habitat. A regular at birdbaths. Visits bird tables, feeding on fatty scraps, bonemeal and mealworms.

Similar species: May occur alongside the Red-capped and White-browed robin-chats in wooded gardens in Nelspruit and White River.

The juvenile Cape Robin-chat (**left**) is heavily spotted and flecked, its plumage helping to camouflage and protect it from potential predators.

RED-CAPPED ROBIN-CHAT

Cossypha natalensis • 18cm

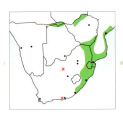

With its glowing orange underparts and silvery back, the striking Red-capped Robin-chat is the subtropical coastal counterpart of the Cape Robin-chat, occurring in well-wooded gardens in Durban and other towns along the south and north coasts of KwaZulu-Natal. Also occurs in the lowveld, usually along rivers and streams, as well as in eastern Zimbabwe. Most active in low light at dawn and dusk, foraging exclusively on the ground. Male and female are alike. Immatures are dark chestnut with buff streaks and spots. Formerly known simply as the Natal Robin.

Feeding: Largely insectivorous, flicking through leaf litter in search of prey such as crickets, roaches, beetles, ants, mantids, spiders and millipedes. Hawks winged termites as they emerge after rain. Less often it feeds on figs and a variety of berries such as those of *Trema*, *Asparagus*, *Scadoxis* and *Dracaena*.

Breeding: Pairs occupy a territory, advertising their presence with constant vocalisations. Prior to breeding, the male performs a tail-raising courtship display. A small bowl-shaped nest of rootlets and other plant material is placed in a crevice or hole of some kind, often close to the ground in a rotted tree stump, or against a fallen branch or rock. The female incubates a clutch of three eggs for 14 days, and the young fledge after a further 14 days.

Voice: The characteristic call is a slurred seesaw whistle, 'tree-turrrr', given mostly at dawn and dusk. This robin-chat is also a superb mimic of other birds' calls, which it weaves into its own repertoire. A single bird may imitate the voices of over 40 species, including raptors, cuckoos, nightjars, bee-eaters and kingfishers.

Left: Like other members in the genus, the juvenile has heavy markings that provide effective camouflage.

Lifespan: Eleven years recorded.

Garden needs: Favours deep shade, tangled thickets and leaf litter, but will occasionally forage on open lawns. Will visit bird tables for mealworms and bonemeal. Drinks and bathes regularly.

Similar species: The Chorister Robin-chat is distinguished by its black head.

WHITE-BROWED ROBIN-CHAT
Cossypha heuglini • **Length: 20cm**

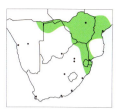

The White-browed Robin-chat is slightly larger and more intensely coloured than its relative the Cape Robin-chat and is restricted to the warmer eastern and northern regions, where it is resident in gardens in Nelspruit, Harare and Maun. The bold white eyebrows are a prominent feature, from which the bird derives its common name. Sexes are alike. This is one of the most vociferous birds in Africa, its loud song being one of the characterstic sounds of riverine woodland and thickets.

Feeding: Largely insectivorous, flicking through leaf litter for crickets, bugs, ants, beetles and spiders. Also takes caterpillars from foliage, and termites from decomposing wood. Occasionally feeds on berries.

Breeding: Pairs occupy a territory throughout the year. A cup-shaped nest of grass, leaf midribs, rootlets and other plant fibres is placed within a cavity such as a hollow tree stump or cleft. The female incubates two eggs for 14 days, and the chicks fledge after about 15 days. Red-chested Cuckoos occasionally parasitise the nests.

Voice: The song is a series of strident whistles, beginning softly and rising to a wild crescendo, with the female joining the male in a duet at the start of the breeding season. A harsh alarm call – 'tserrck-tserrck' – is given when snakes, owls or hawks are present, and in contact with fledglings.

Lifespan: Twelve years recorded.

Garden needs: Favours shaded areas with decomposing leaf litter, but is happy to forage on open lawns and pathways as long as there is cover nearby in which to retreat. Will visit bird tables if mealworms and bonemeal are provided, and drinks and bathes throughout the day.

Similar species: May occur alongside the Cape Robin-chat in well-wooded gardens in Nelspruit and White River.

Formerly known as Heuglin's Robin, this handsome and vociferous bird builds its nest close to the ground, in a hollow tree stump or some man-made site.

BOKMAKIERIE

Telophorus zeylonus • 23cm

The word 'glamorous' seems appropriate when describing the strikingly coloured and unmistakable. Bokmakierie, a bird that visits gardens adjacent to highveld grassland, Karoo scrub, fynbos and strandveld. Typically seen singly or in pairs, it is usually detected by its strident call, which is often given as part of a clear, ringing duet. Male and female are alike, and the immature lacks the bold black throat gorget.

Feeding: Forages mostly on the ground. With its powerful hooked bill, the Bokmakierie can tackle all manner of insects and spiders as well as snails, skinks, dwarf chameleons and even small snakes. It may capture nestlings and small birds, and is known to scavenge from roadkill.

Breeding: Pairs occupy a territory throughout the year. Male and female engage in strident duets, particularly at the onset of the breeding season. A shallow bowl-shaped nest is built out of fine twigs, grass blades and rootlets, and placed in the middle of a leafy shrub or bushy tree. The sexes take turns to incubate the clutch of three eggs for 16 days, and the young fledge after a further 18 days.

Voice: Various loud sounds, such as 'pik-pik-pik-who', 'tleeou-tleeou-tleeo' and 'didlit-didlit-didlit-tring-TRING-TRING', usually in a duet from the top of a bush or fence post. Also gives a variety of other harsh throaty alarm notes.

Lifespan: No data; probably more than eight years.

Garden needs: Rockeries or open areas with widely spaced bushes; will visit or take up residence in gardens alongside natural habitats, but is never wholly suburban. May be lured to a feeding station with mealworms and bonemeal.

Similar species: The Grey-headed Bush-shrike and Orange-breasted Bush-shrike may frequent well-wooded gardens in the warmer eastern and northern parts of the region.

The juvenile Bokmakierie (left) has muted colours and lacks the broad black gorget of the brilliantly coloured adult.

Grey-headed Bush-shrike

SOUTHERN BOUBOU

Laniarius ferrugineus • 22cm

Although it is typically secretive, this bush-shrike can become very bold and tame around people. Invariably seen in pairs, which maintain contact with a variety of crystal-clear piping whistles, while moving through hedges, shrubberies and tree canopies in search of prey. Virtually endemic to South Africa, where it is common around Johannesburg and Cape Town; but it is also present in Gaborone and in southern Mozambique. Five races occur, with variable amounts of white on the male; the female always has more extensive buffy coloration on her underparts.

♂

Feeding: Armed with a hook-tipped bill, this boubou is a predator of large insects, spiders and snails and of small vertebrates such as geckos, skinks, dwarf chameleons, mice and nestling birds. Also takes the eggs of birds and reptiles. Something of a bandit, it may rob thrushes and others of their prey.

Breeding: Pairs defend a territory throughout the year, becoming most vocal and demonstrative prior to breeding. They hop after one another, and perform rapid wing-snapping flight displays, while calling in duet. A shallow bowl made of thin twigs and dry bark is attached to a tangle of small branches in a shaded thicket. Cobwebs are usually used to bind it all together. Both sexes take turns to incubate the clutch of 2–3 eggs for 16 days, and the young leave the nest after a further 16 days. Nests may be parasitised by the Black Cuckoo.

Voice: Highly vocal; its clear, ringing notes drown out the calls of other birds. The male often fans his tail and bobs his head while giving a hollow whistle – 'whoeu-whoeu – bou-bou – whoeu-whoeu-whoue'. A variety of harsh 'tik', 'tuk' and 'tschak' calls are also given.

Lifespan: No data, but probably more than eight years.

Garden needs: Dense shrubberies and tangled thickets; regularly attends birdbaths and will visit bird tables if you provide mealworms or bonemeal.

Similar species: The Tropical Boubou is a common garden bird in Harare and other parts of Zimbabwe.

♀

The female Southern Boubou has more extensive buffy coloration on her underparts than the male.

BLACK-BACKED PUFFBACK

Dryoscopus cubla • **17cm**

Small in size, but demonstrative in nature, this black-and-white bush-shrike draws attention to itself with its loud calls and elaborate flight displays. Occurs throughout the north and east, including the wooded suburbs of Johannesburg, all of Zimbabwe and northern Botswana. Favours leafy tree canopies, but also forages on shaded branches. Pairs or individuals may be seen foraging alongside flycatchers, white-eyes and other species in mixed feeding flocks. The female is duller than the male and has a white line above the eye and bill.

Feeding: Primarily insectivorous, snapping up insects such as bugs, mantids, beetles and caterpillars from the leaves and bark of trees. Also preys on spiders, millipedes and dwarf geckos.

Breeding: Pairs occupy a territory throughout the year. The male performs a dramatic courtship display, starting with a series of loud bill snaps, and then launches himself from his perch in a bouncy, rapid, fluttering flight with erect rump feathers. At this time, the small bird takes on the appearance of a snowball and lives up to its 'puffback' name. The nest is a small, neatly made bowl of petioles and other fine plant fibres, bound to a forked branch with cobwebs. The female incubates a clutch of 2–3 eggs for 14 days, and the young fledge after about 18 days.

Voice: The typical call of the male is a strident 'chick wheeu!' repeated over and over, with the female often joining in duet. Also gives a variety of buzzing alarm calls.

Lifespan: No data, but probably at least six years.

Garden needs: Well-wooded areas with tallish trees in which to forage. The planting of *Acacia*, *Combretum* and *Celtis* will provide foraging opportunities. Rarely, if ever, visits bird tables or birdbaths.

Similar species: The similarly sized Brubru visits gardens in towns in drier bushveld regions, such as Pretoria, Polokwane, Bulawayo and Gaborone.

The male Black-backed Puffback has a completely black crown and erects his white back feathers to create a 'puffball' when displaying; the female is duller with a white supercillium

SOUTHERN FISCAL

Lanius collaris • **22cm**

This is among the best-known and most widespread birds in southern Africa, but it is not the best loved. Although it lacks the hooked claws of a hawk or falcon, the Southern Fiscal is a capable predator of insects and lizards and is also able to kill birds and rodents close to its own weight. Common across the entire region, apart from low-elevation bushveld. The colloquial names 'Butcher Bird' and 'Jacky Hangman' refer to its habit of impaling prey on barbed wire fences or thorn bushes – a larder to which it returns when hungry.

Feeding: Individuals space themselves out, occupying hunting perches from which they can observe and pounce on prey. For this purpose they favour fences, gates, walls and telephone wires over leafy trees and shrubs. Grasshoppers, beetles and small lizards make up the bulk of this shrike's diet, but it will also take rodents, like mice, and smaller birds, like mannikins, when the opportunity arises.

Breeding: Pairs perch prominently to declare their ownership of a territory, chasing off any rivals that might appear. Twigs are collected from the ground and arranged into a sparse bowl or platform in the fork of a tree, usually not too high up. Both sexes incubate a clutch of about three eggs for 25–28 days. Nestlings are fed by both parents and fledge at around 34 days, after which they beg noisily for food.

Voice: The song is a surprisingly melodious jumble of notes, often incorporating some mimicry of other species. The harsh rasping alarm or contact call is more frequently heard.

Lifespan: Up to eight years.

Garden needs: Open areas with walls, fences or posts on which to perch. Will visit bird tables if you provide mealworms or bonemeal. Frequently visits birdbaths.

Similar species: Sometimes confused with the smaller Fiscal Flycatcher (p.93).

The female differs from the male in having buffy patches on her flanks, while the young (**above left**) are finely barred.

COMMON MYNA

Acridotheres tristis • **25cm**

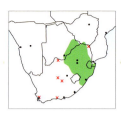

This bird is native to the tropics of Asia (India to Thailand) but was introduced to Durban in around 1900 and to Johannesburg in about 1930, where escaped birds formed free-living feral populations that have since expanded. In all probability, the myna was brought in as a cage bird, since it can be trained to talk. Today, it is a tough and gregarious species that has adapted to human-altered landscapes, flourishing around dockyards, old mines, factories and warehouses, where steel scaffolding and other structures provide ideal nesting conditions and human discards provide food. Usually seen in pairs or small groups, but flocks of thousands may gather at favoured night-time roosts during the winter. Sexes are alike.

Feeding: Feeds on a mix of invertebrates and plant material, taking beetles, cockroaches, snails and spiders, as well as food scraps discarded by people; also feeds on berries such as those of alien *Pyracantha* and *Morus*, and on peaches and corn.

Breeding: Pairs engage in a bowing courtship display with erect crests and fanned tails, while making a metallic swizzling call. The nest comprises a mass of twigs, rags, string, wire, plastic and paper pushed into a cavity, usually a pipe, girder, broken streetlight or electrical box, always well out of reach of humans.

Voice: The typical song is a metallic warble, but it is capable of making many other sounds and can mimic the human voice. The large Hill Myna is usually regarded as the best talking bird in the world and is threatened as a result of the illegal cage-bird trade.

Lifespan: Ringing records are few, but 12–14 years is likely.

Garden needs: Like the Common Starling, this alien bird is not welcomed in most gardens, as it can be aggressive towards other cavity nesters, such as barbets. Because it is often persecuted, it is extremely wary and rarely allows a close approach.

Similar species: None.

As an alien species, the Common Myna is regarded as unwelcome by most people, but, like most invaders, it is simply taking advantage of human modification to the landscape.

COMMON STARLING
Sturnus vulgaris • **21cm**

Native to Europe, but introduced to Cape Town by Cecil John Rhodes in 1889, this starling is now a widespread, invasive species that lives in association with humans in towns and on farms in the southern and eastern Cape. Although generally disliked as a 'messy alien', an unbiased look reveals it to be a striking bird with iridescent plumage. Sexes are alike. Usually seen in small flocks that forage on the ground, they fly up as one to perch in treetops or on fences. Larger flocks assemble in winter, when not breeding, and may perform synchronised flights.

Feeding: Forages mostly on the ground, taking grasshoppers, termites, beetles, ants, spiders, snails and earthworms. Relishes orchard fruit and berries such as those of the alien *Pyracantha*. Also feeds on grain seed, such as wheat, millet and corn. Kitchen scraps and dog pellets are taken when the opportunity arises.

Breeding: In courtship, the male sings at the entrance to a likely nest site, with his nape feathers erected. An untidy bowl of dry grass, twigs, rags, paper and string is wedged into a crevice of some kind – in a wall or eave, in a pipe or in a tree hole made by a woodpecker or barbet. The female incubates a clutch of 4–5 eggs for 15 days, and the nestlings fledge after a further 21 days.

Voice: The male's usual call is a sequence of high-pitched whistles and trills, often given from a rooftop. Also utters a variety of harsh 'karr' alarm notes.

Lifespan: Captive birds have been known to live for up to 20 years.

Garden needs: Open lawns on which to forage, and structures with pipes or cavities in which to nest; because it is an invasive alien, most people are less than enthusiastic about having it around, but it should be remembered that we were the first to invade and modify the natural landscape.

Similar species: None.

Outside the breeding season, both male and female have grey, rather than yellow, bills. The juvenile (**above left**) has a brown head.

VIOLET-BACKED STARLING
Cinnyricinclus leucogaster • 18cm

With his violet-purple head, back and wings with contrasting snow-white underparts, the male is certainly one of the most eye-catching birds in Africa; the colour actually varies from iridescent violet-amethyst to plum-purple, depending on the light. The female, in sharp contrast, resembles a small thrush with brown back and streaked underparts. Usually seen in pairs or small groups, but flocks of 50 or more form after breeding and prior to winter departure. An intra-African migrant, arriving in October and leaving in May, sometimes June.

Feeding: Mostly arboreal, feeding on the berries of trees such as *Apodytes*, *Antidesma*, *Berchemia*, *Boscia*, *Commiphora*, *Phyllanthus* and *Ficus*. Also takes bugs, mantids and caterpillars from foliage and is one of the first birds to appear at termite eruptions, capturing the winged alates in flight.

Breeding: Pairs form upon arrival at the breeding grounds in October. The male gives a squeaky whistled song at the entrance to a potential nest site, while flicking his wings. A shallow cup of grass and twigs, lined with green leaves, is placed within a cavity. A natural tree hole is preferred, but this starling also uses woodpecker holes and upright metal fence poles. The female incubates the clutch of three eggs for 14 days, and the chicks fledge at the age of about 20 days. Nests may be parasitised by the Greater and Lesser honeyguides.

Voice: A soft, drawn-out, whistling 'whoooeu-whiiiuuuuu' is given from a tree canopy or a song post.

Lifespan: No data, but at least 10 years.

Garden needs: Attracted to berry-producing trees as well as fruit on a bird table. May occupy a nest box or log or an upright fence post as a nest site.

Similar species: None.

Male and female are so different that they might be mistaken for entirely different species.

CAPE GLOSSY STARLING
Lamprotornis nitens • **25cm**

One of several iridescent blue starlings, and the most widespread, occurring throughout the region, except, despite its name, in the winter-rainfall regions of the Cape. Usually seen in pairs, but may form small flocks around abundant food sources. It is a cavity nester and seeks out breeding places around human habitation. Male and female are alike. Immatures are dull grey until about six months of age.

Feeding: Like all starlings, it is a mixed feeder, taking all manner of invertebrates, berries, fruit, scraps and the nectar of flowering plants such as *Aloe*, *Schotia*, *Erythrina* and alien *Grevillea*.

Breeding: Places a shallow bowl of grass, plant stems, mammal hair and feathers in a cavity – usually a tree hole made by a barbet or woodpecker; also utilises open pipes and other man-made holes. The female incubates a clutch of three eggs for 16 days, and the young fledge after a further 20 days. The same nest site may be used for several years. May be parasitised by the Great Spotted Cuckoo or Greater Honeyguide.

Voice: The song is a rambling sequence of scratchy whistles.

Lifespan: No records, but at least 10 years.

Garden needs: Berry-producing trees and shrubs may attract this starling, which also comes readily to bird tables where fruit is provided. Will visit birdbaths regularly, especially in hot weather. May use nest boxes and nest logs.

Similar species: The Greater Blue-eared Starling is a common garden bird in the South African lowveld and Zimbabwe, while Burchell's Starling is common in Gaborone, Maun and Windhoek.

Cape Glossy Starlings are generalist feeders that will visit bird tables for fruit or bonemeal as well as taking nectar from flowers.

Burchell's Starling

RED-WINGED STARLING

Onychognathus morio • **30cm**

 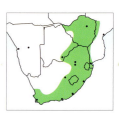

The largest starling in southern Africa, this bird is readily identified by its brick-red primary wing feathers, which are most obvious in flight. Occurs throughout the south and east, but is absent from the semi-arid Karoo and Kalahari, where the smaller Pale-winged Starling replaces it. The female differs from the male in having a pale grey head. Can become quite tame and confiding around people. Typically occurs in pairs or flocks in rocky landscapes but has adapted to nesting and foraging around tall buildings and other human developments.

Feeding: Feeds on the berries of species like *Cussonia* and *Kiggelaria* and of alien plants like *Acacia cyclops* and *Melia azederach*, dispersing their seeds. Relishes the nectar of *Erythrina* and *Aloe* – its face is often yellow with pollen after feeding on these species. Invertebrate prey includes locusts, grasshoppers, termites, beetles, spiders, millipedes, moths and other insects.

Breeding: Pairs occupy a breeding range and tolerate the presence of non-breeding immature birds. Adjacent pairs may nest close together. A bulky bowl of grass, twigs, roots and, sometimes, string and rags is placed in a crevice, on the rafters below an open roof, under an eave or on the frame of a water tank. Three eggs are incubated for 14 days, and the young fledge at about 24 days. Great Spotted Cuckoos may parasitise nests.

Voice: Unlike most starlings, this bird has a beautiful call – a clear, drawn-out 'whu-wheeeeuuo'; also gives a grating alarm call.

Lifespan: Eight years recorded.

Garden needs: Berry-producing trees and shrubs. Readily takes bonemeal and fruit from bird tables.

Similar species: The Pale-winged Starling visits gardens in towns throughout the Karoo and much of Namibia.

The female Red-winged Starling is easily distinguished by her pale, brownish head. This starling takes dead insects from car grills and inspects outdoor braai grids and dog bowls for food. It also hunts for invertebrates around lit buildings after dark. Open-roofed carports may be used for nesting.

Pale-winged Starling

PIED STARLING

Spreo bicolor • **25cm**

A gregarious bird of open country, this starling is common on farmland and along roadsides in South Africa and Lesotho. It often visits gardens in smaller towns across the highveld, Karoo and wheatlands of the southern Cape. The male and female are alike, with distinctive, pale, glowing eyes. Typically seen in small family groups, but flocks of up to a thousand may gather to roost in reedbeds or large *Eucalyptus* trees during winter.

Feeding: Primarily insectivorous, it eats locusts, grasshoppers, termites and especially beetle and fly larvae taken from cowpats. Virtually all food is taken on the ground, but it also rides on livestock, which act as beaters. Figs and berries are relished; also takes kitchen scraps.

Breeding: Forms colonies of 3–20 pairs. Both sexes excavate a tunnel of about 1m in a vertical road cutting or donga wall. The female incubates a clutch of four eggs for 14 days, and the nestlings fledge after a further 25 days. May be parasitised by the Great Spotted Cuckoo.

Great Spotted Cuckoo

Pied Starlings spend most of their time foraging on the ground, picking up insects and grain.

Voice: Not known for its musical ability; gives a rambling sequence of scratchy whistles and warbles.

Lifespan: Eight years recorded.

Garden needs: Will visit bird tables if fruit or bonemeal is provided. Drinks and bathes regularly, so a birdbath may be utilised. Avoids well-wooded areas.

Similar species: None.

CAPE SUGARBIRD

Promerops cafer • ♂ up to 42cm; ♀ up to 26cm

With its extravagant tail feathers, three times the length of its body, the male sugarbird is striking and unmistakable. This species is restricted to the mountainous winter-rainfall areas of the Cape, where it is a regular visitor to gardens from the Cape Peninsula eastwards as far as Port Elizabeth. Usually seen in small groups feeding restlessly around flowering *Protea* and *Leucospermum* species and chasing sunbirds and other Cape Sugarbirds from flower heads. Large flocks form in summer, after breeding.

Feeding: Primarily nectivorous but also snaps up insects, particularly beetles and bees, in flight. Largely dependent on the nectar of various *Protea*, *Leucospermum* and *Mimetes* spp., but seldom, if ever, feeds on *Aloe* nectar. Also visits alien plants like the red-flowered New Zealand Christmas Tree *Metrosideros excelsa* and the Weeping Bottlebrush *Callistemon viminalis*.

Breeding: Pairs occupy a breeding territory, building a bowl-shaped nest of stems, grass and ferns in the centre of a leafy *Protea* or *Leucospermum*. The nest is lined with fluffy seedheads. The female incubates the clutch of two eggs for 17 days, and the young fledge at the age of 18 days. Becomes gregarious after breeding: groups of up to 100 birds feed and roost together.

Voice: The song is a sequence of tinkling and twanging notes, with occasional hisses and musical whistles.

Lifespan: Twelve years recorded.

Garden needs: Mature flowering *Protea* or *Leucospermum* trees will attract these birds from nearby mountain slopes, but they are unlikely to breed in a suburban setting. Will come readily to sugar-water feeders and sliced watermelons.

Similar species: Gurney's Sugarbird is a regular, but seasonal, garden visitor to escarpment towns such as Mashishing (Lydenberg) and Graskop, as well as to parts of the KwaZulu-Natal Midlands and eastern Zimbabwe.

Pincushion Trees (**above left**) and other proteas are the favoured source of nectar for Cape Sugarbirds. Males of this species have extremely long tail feathers.

MALACHITE SUNBIRD

Nectarinia famosa • ♂ up to 24cm; ♀ up to 15cm

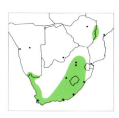

The largest sunbird in southern Africa and certainly one of the region's most spectacular birds. The breeding male is unmistakable, being completely emerald in colour, with long tail streamers. The female is mouse-coloured, darker on the back, with a white outer tail. Occurs in the coastal and mountainous parts of the Cape, through the Karoo and northwards onto the highveld, including in Gauteng. An isolated population occurs in Zimbabwe's Eastern Highlands. Often seen in pairs, the male singing stridently from an exposed perch. At the end of the breeding season, the male's striking plumage fades, then moults, resulting in 'eclipse' plumage for about six months.

Feeding: Mostly nectivorous, but will take invertebrates such as spiders, bugs and beetles when the opportunity arises. Particularly fond of *Aloe* and *Protea* nectar, but will take that of *Leonotis*, *Watsonia*, *Kniphofia* and *Tecoma* and of alien *Grevillea*, *Callistemon* and *Metrosideros*. Moves from one flowering clump to the next in a local circuit, chasing rivals and other sunbird species. Will also visit sugar-water feeders.

Breeding: Pairs form for the breeding cycle only, defending a territory in which the male sings loudly from various prominent perches. In courtship display the male erects yellow 'epaulettes' – small tufts of shoulder feathers. A scruffy purse-shaped nest of fine twiglets, grass and stems is bound to a bush with cobwebs, often above a stream or gulley, and the inside is lined with feathers or plant down. The female incubates two eggs for 14 days, and the nestlings fledge at the age of about 18 days. May be parasitised by Klaas's Cuckoo.

Voice: The male gives a strident swizzling call from a series of prominent song posts, but stops calling once the eggs are laid.

Lifespan: Ten years recorded.

Garden needs: Even a small group of flowering aloes will attract this sunbird during the winter months. Will visit *Tecoma*, *Leonotis* and other flowering plants during summer. Also attracted to sugar-water feeders.

Similar species: None.

The non-breeding male **(above left)** retains some of his iridescent green plumage outside the breeding season; the female has the typical drab plumage of other sunbird species.

WHITE-BELLIED SUNBIRD

Cinnyris talatala • **11cm**

 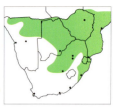

The most common green-backed sunbird in warmer bushveld in the region. It has also expanded its range into Gauteng, probably because of the large number of gardens with flowering plants. The male is a glittering beauty but, as with all sunbirds, the female is drab and mouse-coloured. Usually seen in pairs, often in the company of other nectar-seeking sunbirds and white-eyes.

Feeding: A nectarivore that feeds busily throughout the day at tube-shaped flowers, especially those of *Leonotis*, *Aloe*, *Erythrina*, *Tapinanthus*, *Tecoma*, *Halleria* and *Schotia*, but it feeds just as enthusiastically from aliens such as *Acrocarpus*, *Callistemon*, *Grevillea*, *Eucalyptus* and *Agave*. Captures insects like aphids, ants, flies and beetles and takes spiders from their webs.

Breeding: In display, the male erects 'epaulettes' – small tufts of yellow shoulder feathers. Once the pair is established, the female builds a shaggy, purse-shaped nest using dry stems, grass and leaves, which is usually attached to the tip of a hanging tree branch with cobwebs. On its own, it resembles a clump of plant debris and is superbly camouflaged. The female incubates the clutch of two eggs for 14 days, and the nestlings fledge after a further 14 days.

Voice: The male's song is a sequence of strident musical whistles.

Lifespan: Fifteen years recorded.

Garden needs: A selection of plants with tube-shaped flowers, especially aloes and the Tree Fuchsia *Halleria lucida*, will attract this sunbird. Will also visit sugar-water feeders.

Similar species: The Marico Sunbird is a common garden bird in towns such as Hoedspruit, Gaborone, Maun and Bulawayo.

Marico Sunbird

Males chase and scold rivals in order to establish a breeding territory. This species has been known to build its nest within a spiny cactus, providing defence against would-be nest robbers.

SOUTHERN DOUBLE-COLLARED SUNBIRD

Cinnyris chalybeus • 12cm

This is the most common sunbird in the winter-rainfall region, ever-present in flower gardens along the West Coast, on the Cape Peninsula and eastwards to Port Elizabeth. A tiny but eye-catching bird, with a glittering green head and back and thin scarlet chest band. The female, like other female sunbirds, lacks the bright plumage of the male and is pale olive-brown. A distinct race, with a broader red chest band, occurs in KwaZulu-Natal.

Feeding: A nectarivore that moves restlessly from one plant to the next, frequently chasing rivals, although the larger Malachite Sunbird *Nectarinia famosa* easily intimidates it. Favours *Aloe*, *Erica*, *Halleria*, *Leonotis*, *Salvia* and *Erythrina*, as well as alien *Callistemon*, *Agave* and *Nicotiana*. Also captures invertebrates such as spiders, flies and small beetles.

Breeding: In courtship display, the male erects yellow 'epaulettes' – little tufts of shoulder feathers. Pairs then defend a small territory in which the female builds a scruffy purse-shaped nest out of pliable plant stems, bound with cobwebs to a dense shrub. She incubates a clutch of two eggs for 14 days, and the young fledge after a further 16 days.

Voice: Gives whispy, tinkling notes from a perch. Noisier in winter and prior to egg laying.

Lifespan: Nine years recorded.

Garden needs: A selection of aloes and other plants with tube-shaped flowers, especially *Leonotis*, *Erica*, *Salvia* and *Halleria*. Also visits artificial sugar-water feeders.

Similar species: The Greater Double-collared Sunbird may occur alongside the Southern in coastal gardens from Hermanus to Durban, and in escarpment towns such as Graskop; the longer, less curved bill is a distinguishing feature.

Greater Double-collared Sunbird

These tiny sunbirds visit nectar-producing flowers throughout the year, favouring aloes, pincushions and proteas.

SCARLET-CHESTED SUNBIRD
Chalcomitra senegalensis • 14cm

The first impression is of a jet-black bird with a blood-red chest patch, but in good light the plumage is actually dark velvety brown. Either way, the male is a dazzling creature, usually seen alone or in the company of his mate. In southern Africa, this bird is confined to warm bushveld, and is a regular visitor to gardens in Polokwane, Nelspruit, Bulawayo and Harare. The female lacks the male's bright coloration, and is darker than the similarly sized female Amethyst Sunbird.

Feeding: A nectarivore that uses its curved bill to probe the tube-shaped flowers of *Erythrina*, *Tapinanthus*, *Schotia*, *Leonotis*, *Kigelia* and *Aloe* species. Often feeds alongside other types of sunbird and is typically dominant. Insects such as ants, aphids and beetles are taken from flowers, while spiders may be snatched from their webs.

Breeding: The male defends his breeding territory aggressively and displays to his mate with a swaying head-bowing display. The female uses dry stems and leaves to build a purse-shaped nest, typically bound with cobwebs to the end of a hanging tree branch, although it is sometimes suspended from an overhead wire or pergola. The interior is lined with feathers, hair and plant down, while the exterior is usually camouflaged with bits of lichen and bark to resemble windblown debris. The female incubates the clutch of two eggs for 14 days, and the young leave the nest after a further 17 days.

Voice: The male's song is a strident 'chip-chip-CHIP-chip', repeated from a treetop perch for lengthy periods.

Lifespan: Nine years recorded.

Garden needs: Planting a selection of aloes is the easiest way to attract this species, with *Aloe chabaudii* being a particular favourite. A mature *Erythrina* or *Schotia* tree in flower will almost certainly lure this bird to your garden.

Similar species: None.

The male Scarlet-chested Sunbird is one of the region's most eye-catching birds, but the female is drably coloured, as is the case with most others in the family.

AMETHYST SUNBIRD
Chalcomitra amethystine • **14cm**

The male of this large sunbird species appears black but is actually dark velvety brown, like the male of the closely related Scarlet-chested Sunbird. His iridescent throat patch is a dazzling amethyst in sunlight, and the crown a glowing emerald. The female, as is typical of females in this family, has plain plumage. Usually seen singly, or in pairs, often alongside other sunbirds at abundant nectar sources. Common over the wetter eastern and northern parts of southern Africa, but has expanded its range westwards to the Cape Peninsula in recent years.

Feeding: Largely nectivorous, using its curved bill to probe the flowers of *Halleria*, *Erythrina*, *Kigelia* and *Tecoma* trees as well as those of smaller plants including *Aloe*, *Kniphofia* and *Strelitzia*. Also happy to feed from aliens such as *Acrocarpus* and *Callistemon*, and will visit sugar-water feeders, where it bosses other birds.

Breeding: The male aggressively defends a breeding territory and engages in high-speed chases with his mate prior to egg laying. The female builds a shaggy, purse-shaped nest out of dry grass, fine twigs and stems, which is bound with cobwebs to the end of a drooping branch and camouflaged with lichen and dry leaves. Sometimes builds the nest on a telephone wire, washing line or other man-made structure.

Voice: The male sings from an exposed perch, giving a high-pitched, chattering 'keep-keep-kyip-keep', sometimes continuously for long periods.

Lifespan: Eight years recorded.

Garden needs: Planting a selection of aloes is the easiest way to attract this species, with *Aloe arborescens* being a favourite. A mature *Halleria* or *Erythrina* tree in flower will almost certainly lure this bird if it occurs naturally in your district.

Similar species: None.

The nest (**above right**) is a small purse-shaped pouch, camouflaged with lichen and suspended from the end of a twig to resemble windblown plant debris.

COLLARED SUNBIRD
Hedydipna collaris • **10cm**

 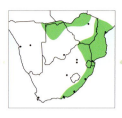

This tiny sunbird differs from other local members of the family in that its bill is short and only slightly decurved, and the female is almost as brightly coloured as the male. Restricted to the warmer eastern and northern parts of southern Africa, it occurs in thorny savanna, coastal forest and valley thicket and is a familiar garden bird in East London, Durban, Pietermaritzbrg and Nelspruit. Usually seen foraging in pairs or within a mixed feeding group.

Feeding: Takes far more insects and spiders than do other sunbirds, its shorter bill being ideal for gleaning aphids and ants and snapping up flies and small moths. Relishes the nectar of *Aloe*, *Albizia*, *Combretum*, *Burchellia*, *Halleria* and *Strelitzia* and will 'steal' nectar from Sausage Tree *Kigelia africana* and other large bell-shaped flowers by piercing the back of the flower.

Breeding: Pairs defend a territory vigorously, often 'boxing' their own reflections in windows, and may enter houses to take on 'rivals' at mirrors! The male gives a bowing courtship display, hopping back and forth on a branch as his mate watches. The female builds a small oval nest using dry stems, leaves and bark strips and lines it with fluffy plant down. The nest is attached to a twig out in the open, often close to a building or active paper wasps' nest, which acts as a deterrent to predators. The female incubates 2–3 eggs for 14 days, and the chicks fledge after a further 14 days. May be parasitised by Klaas's Cuckoo.

Voice: Male gives a high-pitched rattling trill.

Lifespan: Eleven years recorded.

Garden needs: Favours tall trees, dense cover and flowering plants, especially the Flame Creeper *Combretum microphyllum*.

This species is unique among local sunbirds, in that the female's plumage is almost as bright as that of the male.

Similar species: The Variable Sunbird is a common garden bird in Harare; it has a much longer bill than the Collared Sunbird.

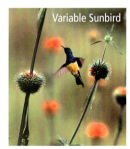

Variable Sunbird

CAPE WHITE-EYE
Zosterops capensis • 12cm

Common and widespread, this is one of the most familiar garden birds in South Africa. There are four races, which are best distinguished by the colour of their underparts. These little green birds are immediately recognised by the ring of tiny white feathers around their eyes. Usually seen in pairs or small parties, but flocks of up to 50 may congregate in winter. The sexes are alike in appearance. White-eyes are often so engrossed in their foraging that they appear not to notice human observers.

Z. c. capensis

Feeding: A mixed feeder, taking berries and insects; something of an aphid specialist and should be valued by gardeners of roses and other ornamental plants. Forages by inspecting the undersides of leaves, flower buds and bark, often hanging upside down to seize small insects. Frequently joined by mixed feeding flocks including orioles, flycatchers and woodpeckers. Favours the berries of *Kiggelaria*, *Antidesma* and *Trema*, ripe figs and the fruits of invasive alien plants such as Brazilian Pepper Tree *Schinus molle* and Yellow Firethorn *Pyracantha angustifolia*. Relishes the nectar of *Aloe*, *Strelitzia* and *Erythrina*, among others.

Breeding: A small cup nest made of dry bark strips, grass and rootlets is slung between two branchlets hammock-style using cobwebs; may also use string and wool near human settlements. Both sexes help to incubate the clutch of 2–3 eggs for 10–12 days, and the young fledge after a further 12 days.

Voice: The song is a series of soft but distinctive tinkling whistles, often incorporating the calls of other species. These contact calls keep the foraging flock together.

Lifespan: Twelve years recorded.

Garden needs: Drinks and bathes regularly, and makes good use of birdbaths. Berry-bearing trees will attract feeding groups.

Similar species: The Orange River White-eye is a common garden bird in Bloemfontein and Kimberely; the African Yellow White-eye in Harare and Bulawayo.

Z. c. caniviridis

In the southern Cape, the Cape White-eye has contrasting grey underparts **(above)**, while populations in other parts of the region have greenish-yellow underparts **(left)**.

HOUSE SPARROW
Passer domesticus • **14cm**

Native to Eurasia, the House Sparrow has followed people around the world, initially establishing feral populations at ports and coastal towns then moving inland via railway routes. Most introductions were deliberate, as colonisers wished to have familiar creatures around them, but others arrived accidentally via large ships on which the birds had nested. As with the House Mouse and House Rat, it is now seemingly dependent on humans and is rarely found in undisturbed habitats. Usually seen in pairs or small gatherings, often with other granivores. The male is more boldly coloured than the female, with a black mask and bib.

Feeding: Eats seeds, all manner of human food scraps and crumbs, as well as flower buds, fruit, small invertebrates and snails' eggs.

Breeding: The breeding cycle usually begins in September. An untidy ball of dry grass, weeds, string, rags and plastic is built within a cavity in an eave, pipe, broken signpost, streetlight or abandoned vehicle. Both sexes incubate the clutch of four eggs for 13 days, and the young usually fledge after a further 18 days.

Voice: The vocal repertoire is limited to a series of cheerful chirps, repeated with variations.

Lifespan: Eight years recorded.

Garden needs: Will visit feeding stations if seed is provided, and will explore cavities as potential nesting sites. As an alien species, the House Sparrow is not always cherished, but is so hardy and adaptable that it can provide cheer and interest wherever it is seen.

Similar species: The Great Sparrow visits gardens in Kimberley, Gaborone and Windhoek.

The male House Sparrow has a grey crown and white cheeks, whereas the female lacks these features.

CAPE SPARROW

Passer melanurus • 16cm

Occurring throughout South Africa (where it is absent only from the lowveld and the humid coast of northern KwaZulu-Natal), as well as in Namibia and southern Botswana, the Cape Sparrow is one of the most familiar birds. Although adapted to semi-arid and even desert conditions, this sparrow thrives around humans and their settlements, finding food and nesting sites in suburbs and towns and on farms. Males are distinguished from females by their bold black-and-white facial pattern. Usually seen in pairs or small flocks, often feeding on the ground with other granivores.

Feeding: The seeds of grasses and weedy forbs comprise its main diet, but it also eats flower buds, fruit and nectar. Picks up scraps and crumbs on pathways and along roadsides. Termites and small beetles are among its invertebrate prey.

Breeding: The breeding cycle begins in August or September. A scruffy ball of grass stems lined with feathers and plant down is placed in a thorny tree or in a man-made structure such as an eave, a drainpipe against a wall, a nest box or the mud nest of a swallow or martin. String, rags, wool and other debris may be used when available. The clutch of 3–4 eggs is incubated by both sexes for 12–14 days, with the young fledging at around 17 days. Nests may be parasitised by the Diederik Cuckoo.

Voice: Usually just a series of scratchy chirps, but males also have a rippling, high-pitched song.

Lifespan: Ten years recorded.

Garden needs: Will visit feeding stations where seed is provided, and is a regular at birdbaths. Will explore cavities as potential nesting sites. Likes to dust bathe, so an area of exposed sand may prove popular.

Similar species: None.

The male Cape Sparrow has a bold head and throat pattern, while the female is more subdued in appearance.

SOUTHERN GREY-HEADED SPARROW

Passer diffusus • **15cm**

Lacking the bold facial patterns of the male Cape and House sparrows, this widespread bird often goes undetected in gardens, or is mistaken for the female of one of the more familiar sparrow species. The sexes are alike, with a plain grey head and underparts. The bill is dark grey when breeding, but horn-coloured in winter. In southern Africa it is absent only from the arid succulent Karoo. Invariably seen in pairs, but will feed alongside other granivores.

Feeding: Collects the seeds of grasses and herbs from the ground, including those of the invasive Paperthorn *Alternanthera pungens*. Also eats the small berries of *Lycium* and *Searsia*, takes fallen figs and sips on aloe nectar. Termites and small beetles are among its invertebrate prey.

Breeding: The breeding cycle usually begins in November, but eggs may be laid in any month. Unlike other native sparrows, it is a cavity nester, choosing a natural hollow in a tree or a hole made by a woodpecker or barbet. It may also use the mud-pellet nest of a swallow, a nesting box or a hollow fence post.

Voice: Not known for its fine voice, the male calls by giving a series of simple chirps from a prominent perch.

Lifespan: Six years recorded.

Garden needs: Will frequent a birdbath for refreshment. May be attracted to a nest box, but will have to compete with larger and more aggressive barbets and starlings, among others.

Similar species: Sometimes confused with the Lesser Honeyguide (p.74), but that bird has olive-green upperparts.

The juvenile (**left**) displays the fleshy gape characteristic of so many birds that have recently left the nest.

WHITE-BROWED SPARROW-WEAVER
Plocepasser mahali • **17cm**

A noisy and gregarious bird of the Kalahari and drier western regions, this sparrow-weaver is common in open parks and gardens in towns such as Kimberley, Bloemfonten, Polokwane, Windhoek, Gaborone and Bulawayo. Where it does occur, it is usually abundant and its large straw nests are always conspicuous. The prominent white supercilium and snow-white rump are distinctive features that immediately separate if from any of the sparrows. Always seen in small flocks, usually numbering no more than 20 individuals.

Feeding: Small flocks feed on the ground, collecting fallen seeds and turning over pebbles and dung to capture beetles, termites and other invertebrates.

Breeding: A cooperative breeder. A dominant pair is assisted by up to five nest helpers. Each family builds about 10 or 12 nests of straw on the outer branches of a thorn tree, but only one nest is used for breeding, the others serving as sleeping chambers. Nests are usually clustered on the western side of the tree (away from prevailing winds) and are built of dry grass and lined with feathers. The female incubates the clutch of two eggs for 14 days. Nestlings are fed by the parents and their helpers, and fledge at about 22 days.

Voice: Very vocal, engaging in noisy bouts of sharp but musical high-pitched warbles and squeaks.

Lifespan: Ten years recorded.

Garden needs: Will visit gardens adjacent to open areas, especially if thorn trees are available for nesting. Will regularly visit bird tables and birdbaths.

Similar species: None.

The male White-browed Sparrow-weaver has a dark bill, whereas the female's is horn-coloured.

SCALY-FEATHERED FINCH
Sporopipes squamifrons • 10cm

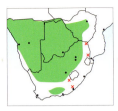

With its powder-pink bill and black 'handlebar' moustache, this tiny finch is quite unmistakable, occurring in the semi-arid western parts of southern Africa, where it is a regular visitor to, or inhabitant of, gardens in towns such as Kimberley, Gaborone and Windhoek. The small black feathers of the crown are edged with white and resemble scales, the feature for which this little bird was named. Males and females are alike. Usually seen in pairs or small groups.

Feeding: Seeds of grasses and herbs are collected on the ground or from seedheads. Often feeds in the company of waxbills, sparrows and other granivores. Termites and small beetles are among its invertebrate prey.

Breeding: The breeding cycle usually begins in January, but nesting has been recorded in all months. A scruffy ball-shaped nest of dry grass stems, often lined with guineafowl feathers, is built deep within a thorny tree. Both sexes incubate the clutch of four eggs for 12 days, and the young usually fledge after a further 16 days. The nest is used as a sleeping chamber throughout the year.

Voice: Not vociferous, just a series of whispy chirps.

Lifespan: Four years recorded.

Garden needs: Open areas for foraging. Will take seeds scattered on the ground or placed on a bird table. Thorn trees are used for nesting. Will frequent a birdbath.

Similar species: The much larger Sociable Weaver regularly visits gardens in Kimberley, Upington and throughout most of Namibia.

The Scaly-feathered Finch forages and nests in thorn trees, in pairs or family groups.

Sociable Weaver

RED-HEADED FINCH

Amadina erythrocephala • **11cm**

This small gregarious finch is often nomadic, moving to wherever food is available, which depends on summer rainfall patterns. Populations periodically irrupt and move into suitable habitat outside of the usual range. Some populations appear to be more sedentary, establishing themselves in suburban areas where food and water are available year-round. Only the male sports the dark red hood, but the scaly barred underparts of both sexes distinguish this species from sparrows and firefinches. A frequent visitor to gardens in Bloemfontein, Pretoria and parts of Johannesburg, often from nearby farmlands.

Feeding: Usually collects the seeds of grasses and herbs from the ground, often feeding in the company of sparrows and other granivores. Will also perch on seedheads to strip them. Often visits garden feeding stations where seeds are provided, and drinks and bathes regularly. Termites and small beetles are among its invertebrate prey.

Breeding: The breeding cycle usually begins in February, but nesting has been recorded in all months. Instead of building its own nest, the Red-headed Finch typically occupies the disused nest of a weaver or, less often, a sparrow. The clutch of four eggs is incubated by both sexes for 12–14 days, with young fledging at around 20 days.

Voice: A series of buzzing notes or nasal chirps.

Lifespan: Four years recorded.

Garden needs: Likes bare ground or clipped lawn and becomes a regular at feeding stations where seed is provided. Will frequent a birdbath for drinking and bathing.

Similar species: The Cut-throat Finch favours warmer bushveld regions, but sometimes occurs alongside the Red-headed Finch in Johannesburg and Pretoria gardens; there are records of hybridisation.

The Red-headed Finch may use boxes or other man-made objects for nesting (**left**).

Cut-throat Finch

137

VILLAGE WEAVER
Ploceus cucullatus • 16cm

Formerly known as the Spotted-backed Weaver, a name that aptly describes the distinctive black-and-yellow mantle of the breeding male. This is a common weaver in the warmer northern and eastern parts of southern Africa, where it forms large and noisy breeding colonies in summer. The female closely resembles the female Southern Masked Weaver but has red, not brown, eyes.

Feeding: Probably consumes more seeds than insects, except when feeding young. Takes grain and grass seeds from the ground or by stripping stems. Relishes the nectar of, among others, *Aloe*, *Erythrina* and *Schotia*, and feeds on flower petals and parts. Termites, ants and small beetles are among the insects taken.

Breeding: Polygynous; males mate with up to five females per season. The breeding season usually starts in September, but some individuals begin earlier. Males occupy and defend sites within a colony, sometimes numbering hundreds of birds, most often situated in trees above water. The male builds several nests, some of which will be accepted by females. Each female incubates a clutch of 2–3 eggs for 12 days, and the nestlings fledge at around 19 days. The Diederik Cuckoo is a persistent and cunning brood parasite, so the weavers must remain vigilant.

Voice: A series of metallic buzzing and rasping sounds, given most often by the male when hanging from a newly constructed nest, trying to draw attention to what he has created.

Lifespan: Fourteen years recorded (but up to 24 years in captivity).

Garden needs: Seeds, aloes and nectar-bearing trees. Pendulous branches above a pond or wetland may attract breeding males.

Similar species: The Southern and Lesser masked weavers featured opposite.

Flowering *Erythrina* trees attract Village Weavers to their nectar.

SOUTHERN MASKED WEAVER
Ploceus velatus • **15cm**

This is the most widespread of all southern African weavers, occurring across the entire region, and most gardens are visited or inhabited by these adaptable birds. The breeding male may be confused with the Village Weaver (opposite), but the black back of the latter distinguishes it. The female closely resembles the female Village Weaver but has brown, not red, eyes. Usually seen in small groups.

Feeding: Seeds probably feature more often than insects do in its diet, except when feeding young. Takes grain and grass seeds from the ground or by stripping stems. Also feeds on small seeds, pine nuts and berries, petals and, sometimes, nectar. Termites and small beetles are among the insects taken.

Breeding: Polygynous; males mate with up to five females per season. They usually begin breeding in September, but some start much earlier. Males may nest alone or within a colony, usually in a large tree overhanging water, but sometimes in a lone-standing tree in scrub or grassland, or even on a wire fence strand over water. The male builds several nests, some of which will be accepted by females. The female incubates a clutch of 2–3 eggs for 12–14 days, and the nestlings fledge at around 17 days. Breeding weavers must always be on guard for the Diederik Cuckoo, a persistent and cunning brood parasite.

Voice: Mechanical swizzling sounds, higher pitched than those of the Cape Weaver.

Lifespan: Thirteen years recorded.

Garden needs: Bird tables with seeds, and birdbaths for drinking and bathing. A tree in which to nest.

Although they will breed in any kind of tree, breeding males can seldom resist a tree with branches hanging above a pond or wetland.

Similar species: The Lesser Masked Weaver has grey, not pink, legs and feet, with the male having distinctive pale eyes.

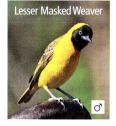

Lesser Masked Weaver

CAPE WEAVER
Ploceus capensis • 18cm

This is the largest weaver in South Africa and, lacking any black facial markings, it is easily separated from the three common masked weavers that also frequent suburban gardens across the highveld, Karoo and southern Cape. As with other weavers, the male assumes bright breeding plumage, at which time he looks completely different from the drab female. The pale eyes and dagger-shaped bill give this weaver a rather fierce appearance.

Feeding: Eats seeds and insects in equal amounts, taking most of its food from the ground. Also uses its pointed bill to extract beetle larvae and other insects from tree bark. This weaver is very fond of aloe nectar.

Breeding: Polygynous; males mate with up to seven females per season. In the southwestern Cape the breeding cycle begins in July; birds on the highveld usually begin breeding in August. Males form a small colony in a large tree or, less often, a reedbed, and each male defends a small territory in which he builds several nests, some of which will be accepted by females. Each female incubates a clutch of 2–3 eggs for 12–14 days, and nestlings fledge at around 17 days.

Voice: A sequence of rasping, mechanical-sounding swizzles, deeper than the vocalisations of the Southern Masked Weaver.

Lifespan: Eight years recorded.

Garden needs: Visits bird tables where seeds are provided, and drinks and bathes at birdbaths. Almost any sizeable tree may be considered as a nesting site, but one with pendulous branches above a pond or wetland is often irresistible

Observing a weaver building its intricate hanging nest leaves human observers full of admiration, although some bemoan the birds' habit of stripping palm fronds and other leaves from their precious plants.

Similar species: The African (Holub's) Golden Weaver is its lowveld counterpart, but the species occur alongside one another in Nelspruit and White River.

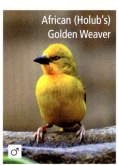

African (Holub's) Golden Weaver

THICK-BILLED WEAVER
Amblyospiza albifrons • **18cm**

A large, heavy-billed, sexually dimorphic weaver. Formerly restricted to the warmer northeastern parts of southern Africa, it has extended its range in the past few decades and now occurs on the highveld, including throughout much of Gauteng. The breeding male is dark chocolate-brown with a snow-white forehead and white wing panels. The female is paler brown, with brown-streaked white underparts and an ochre-yellow bill. Usually seen in small flocks of 8–20 birds.

Feeding: The massive bill is used to crack the seeds of small fruits, especially those of the White Stinkwood *Celtis Africana* and Thorny Elm *Chaetacme aristata*. Flocks may gather in Sunflower *Helianthus annuus* plantations to forage on the seeds. Other berries taken include Wild Peach *Kiggelaria africana* and the invasive Syringa *Melia azederach*.

Breeding: Polygynous; males mate with several females each season. The breeding season usually starts in October. Males occupy and defend sites within a colony, but some individuals may nest alone. The male builds several nests, the most finely woven and attractive built by any local weaver, between two vertical stems of *Typha* bulrush or *Phragmites* reeds. Some nests are accepted by females, and the clutch of three eggs is incubated for 15 days. Nestlings fledge at around 20 days.

Voice: Unusually quiet for a weaver. The male does little more than chatter and trill and gives the occasional high-pitched whistle. Individuals and flocks are often detected by the snapping sound as birds break into hard seeds.

Lifespan: Nine years recorded.

Garden needs: Mature White Stinkwood trees will attract this weaver. Small wetlands with *Typha* bulrushes may be used as nesting sites.

Similar species: None.

The female is distinguished by her yellow, cone-shaped bill and streaky underparts. The male is dark chocolate brown with white wing patches, and is responsible for the finely woven nest.

RED-BILLED QUELEA
Quelea quelea • 12cm

Foraging in swarms of millions and breeding in enormous colonies, these small sparrow-like birds have been called 'feathered locusts' and are the most abundant bird species not only in southern Africa, but in the rest of the continent too. This quelea may even be the most abundant bird on Earth, and grain farmers regard it as a plague. Favours bushveld regions but may be spreading southwards. Females and non-breeding males resemble sparrows or weavers but have a wax-red bill and eye ring and pink-orange legs. Breeding males have a black mask and a variety of facial patterns, even within the same regional population. Largely absent from the winter-rainfall region.

Feeding: Feeds on the seeds of grains and wild grasses and damages crops of millet, sorghum, oats, rice and wheat. Flocks feed with a unique rolling motion – the birds from the back continually flying over those at the front.

Breeding: The breeding cycle is erratic and follows rainfall patterns, but generally takes place from January to March. Hundreds of thousands of birds form a colony, usually weaving their weaver-like nests in thorn trees. The nesting cycle is very rapid, with both parents incubating the eggs for 10–12 days, and the young fledging after a further 10–13 days. Colonies are extremely noisy and attract many predators including eagles, kites, hawks, storks, mongooses and snakes.

Voice: Gives a short, sharp chatter and a high whistle.

Lifespan: Eight years recorded.

Garden needs: Individuals or small groups may visit bird tables provisioned with fine seed.

Similar species: Females and non-breeding males may be confused with the smaller females of the Pin-tailed Whydah and Village Indigobird, which also have red bills.

In garden situations, the Red-billed Quelea is never as gregarious or abundant as when flocking in natural savanna or bushveld.

SOUTHERN RED BISHOP

Euplectes orix • **13cm**

 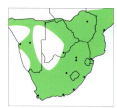

Perched on a fence or bursting up from a verge, this is one of the most striking and noticeable of southern African birds – but only in the summer breeding season. The males lose their brilliant vermillion-and-black plumage in winter and then resemble the drab sparrow-like hens. Southern Red Bishops occur throughout the region, except for the northern Kalahari and most of Namibia. As agriculture and irrigation have expanded, this gregarious little bird has expanded its range across South Africa, and populations have increased in size. It visits gardens close to open areas or to the reedbeds in which it breeds. Usually seen in small groups, but large flocks assemble in winter.

Feeding: Consumes the seeds of various wild and cultivated grass species, including those of commercial crops. The seeds are picked off the ground or stripped from stems. Termites and other small insects are taken when available to provision nestlings.

Breeding: Polygynous; males mate with several females each season. The breeding season is usually under way by September. The males typically occupy and defend sites within a colony (although some individuals nest alone) and tend to space themselves further apart than do colonial weavers. Each male builds an average of eight loosely woven nests between the upright stems of reeds. Females accept some of the nests, and a clutch of three eggs is incubated for 13 days. Nestlings fledge at around 14 days. Nests are frequently parasitised by Diederik Cuckoos.

Voice: The male gives an insect-like buzzing song, usually with the feathers of his mantle and neck raised. He buzzes back and forth in noisy display at his small breeding territory.

Lifespan: Seventeen years recorded.

Garden needs: May visit feeding stations where fine seed is provided, and may nest in bulrushes planted in wetlands.

Similar species: None, but females may be confused with non-breeding weavers and other bishops.

Outside of the breeding season, male bishops assume the drab plumage of the females.

BRONZE MANNIKIN
Lonchura cucullata • **9cm**

 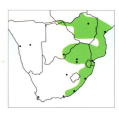

Resembling a miniature sparrow, this tiny bird is usually seen in family groups or flocks of up to 30. Sexes are alike. It occurs in the warmer northern and eastern parts of southern Africa. It has also expanded its range onto the highveld, where agriculture and urban settlements provide suitable habitat, and is now a common garden bird in many parts of Gauteng. In some regions it forms mixed flocks with the Red-backed Mannikin.

Feeding: Forages mostly on the ground, keeping to the shade where possible, to pick up fallen grass seeds. Like other small granivores, it flies up to perch on a seeding stem, which sinks to the ground under the bird's weight and is then stripped. Sometimes eats the petals and nectar of various flowers, and will take termites and other small invertebrates.

Breeding: Breeding season usually begins in November. In courtship, the male holds a grass stem in his bill and bobs on a branch for his mate. A ball-shaped nest of fine grass stems is built within a tangle of thorny branches, usually about 4m off the ground; sometimes uses an old weaver's nest. The clutch of 4–5 eggs is incubated by both sexes for 14 days, and the young fledge after 17 days. The nests are occasionally parasitised by Pin-tailed Whydahs.

Voice: A series of soft, jumbled, tinkling notes.

Lifespan: Three years recorded.

Garden needs: Prefers areas of rank growth with seeding grasses and may appear if lawns are allowed to go to seed. Quick to visit feeding tables with fresh seed; a birdbath will also attract these mannikins.

Similar species: The Red-backed Mannikin visits gardens from Port Elizabeth to Durban, as well as Nelspruit, sometimes feeding alongside the Bronze Mannikin.

Moving busily about in tight flocks, little Bronze Mannikins are entertaining birds to watch in the garden. The juvenile (**left**) is plain cinnamon-brown.

PIN-TAILED WHYDAH

Vidua macroura • 12cm (plus tail of up to 22cm in breeding ♂)

The behaviour of this tiny streamer-tailed granivore gives gardeners plenty to talk about. The males assume their pied plumage and long tails at the start of the breeding season, occupying a display site, which is usually located near a regular supply of seeds or water, very often in a suburban garden. The pugnacious males then aggressively chase away rivals as well as other species while courting and mating with female whydahs that visit to feed or drink. Females and non-breeding males resemble tiny sparrows, but with a bold black-and-buff striped head and pink bill.

Feeding: Grass seeds are taken on the ground or from seedheads. Often feeds in the company of waxbills and other granivores.

Breeding: A brood parasite that lays its eggs in the nests of Common Waxbills or, occasionally, those of other small finches. The male performs at a display site, mating with numerous females, each of which will lay an average of 25 eggs over the season, placing just one egg at a time in the nest of a waxbill host. The egg hatches after 11 days, before the waxbill's own eggs hatch, and is then fed by the foster parents.

Voice: A series of squeaky metallic whistles – 'peetzy, weetzy, weetzy'.

Lifespan: Six years recorded.

Garden needs: Quick to come to a feeding station where seed is provided. If you want the territorial male to depart, your only option is to stop putting out seeds and to turn your feeding table over to frugivores or insectivores.

Similar species: The Shaft-tailed Whydah visits gardens in dry bushveld regions and may be a common garden bird in towns such as Kimberley, Gaborone, Bulawayo and Windhoek.

Watching Pin-tailed Whydahs in your garden is fascinating, although these aggressive little birds may discourage other species from visiting feeding stations.

BLUE WAXBILL
Uraeginthus angolensis • 12cm

This tiny powder-blue bird occurs in the warmer northern and eastern parts of southern Africa, where it is a familiar garden bird in towns such as Hoedspruit, Polokwane, Maun, Bulawayo and Harare. The male is brighter than the female, with more extensive blue on the flanks. Usually seen in pairs but may form small flocks when not breeding. Not as restless as other waxbills, sometimes feeding on the ground close to people. Interestingly, and no doubt as a means of avoiding detection by hunting raptors, ground-feeding waxbills often follow the shadows cast by trees.

Feeding: Forages mostly on the ground, keeping to the shade where possible, to pick up fallen grass seeds. Like other small granivores, these waxbills perch on a seeding stem, which sinks to the ground under the bird's weight and is then stripped.

Breeding: Breeding usually begins in January, but has been recorded throughout the year. In courtship, the male holds a long grass stem in his bill and bobs up and down on a horizontal branch in front of his mate. A ball-shaped nest of grass stems is built within a tangle of thorny branches. Both sexes incubate the clutch of four eggs for 12 days, and the young fledge at around 17 days. The Shaft-tailed Whydah occasionally parasitises this waxbill's nests.

Voice: A whispy, high-pitched buzz, given from the canopy of a bush or small tree.

Lifespan: Twelve years recorded.

Garden needs: Rank growth such as a lawn gone to seed. Quick to visit feeding tables with fresh seed, and may visit a birdbath.

Similar species: None. The closely related Green-winged Pytilia is a common garden visitor in bushveld towns, including parts of Pretoria and Bulawayo.

Green-winged Pytilia

Blue Waxbills favour areas of rank growth with seeding grasses. They often nest near to an active paper wasps' nest. The wasps aggressively defend their own nest from monkeys and thus protect the waxbills too.

COMMON WAXBILL
Estrilda astrild • **12cm**

This tiny bird, with its lipstick-red bill and mask, is the most widespread member of its family in southern Africa, occurring everywhere except in the Kalahari, and patchily throughout Namibia. Typically a bird of marshes and wetlands, its distribution range has probably expanded with the spread of irrigated farms, and it readily visits gardens where seed and water are provided. Usually seen in small, tight flocks of six or seven individuals, but larger groups aggregate in winter. The sexes are alike.

Feeding: Ripe seeds are stripped from grass stems or collected on the ground. If disturbed, will fly up into trees or reeds, usually returning after a short while. Often feeds and drinks alongside mannikins or other waxbills.

Breeding: The breeding season begins in August or September in the southern Cape, but later in the summer-rainfall regions. Pairs may be faithful to one another but only defend the nest site itself. In courtship, the male holds a long grass stem and fluffs out his feathers to expose the red underbelly to his mate. A scruffy pouch-like nest of dry grass is built within tangled vegetation close to the ground. Both sexes incubate the clutch of 4–6 eggs for 12 days, and the young fledge after a further 17–21 days. The Pin-tailed Whydah regularly parasitises this waxbill's nest.

Voice: A feeding flock maintain contact with bursts of soft whistles. Gives a distinctive 'pjink-pjink' call in flight.

Lifespan: Nine years recorded.

Garden needs: Areas of rank growth with seeding grasses. Visits birdbaths and frequents feeding tables with fresh seed.

Similar species: The Swee Waxbill regularly visits gardens in the southern Cape and the wetter, eastern parts of South Africa.

Swee Waxbill

Moving about in small, busy flocks Common Waxbills enliven the garden. In other parts of the world they are popular cage birds, but escaped individuals have formed feral populations.

YELLOW-FRONTED CANARY

Crithagra mozambicus • 12cm

This is the most common canary in the more wooded northern and eastern parts of South Africa, Zimbabwe and Botswana. The male has bright lemon-yellow underparts and supercilium, an olive-green back and a grey nape. The female is duller, with a paler underbelly, and the juvenile is lightly streaked. Usually seen in pairs or small family groups, but may form larger flocks in winter. The male sings sweetly from treetops. These canaries feed on lawns and clearings alongside sparrows and weavers; when disturbed, they call softly as they fly up from the ground and perch in nearby trees, before departing or returning to the ground.

Feeding: Collects the seeds of grasses and herbs from the ground or takes them from seedheads. Often feeds alongside waxbills and other granivores. Termites and other small insects are taken when the opportunity arises and are actively sought out for feeding to the young. Also relishes the nectar of *Erythrina* and the flower parts of *Combretum*.

Breeding: Breeding cycle usually begins in November. A small cup-shaped nest is built with fine stems, rootlets and grass, on an outer branch of a dense bush or small tree. The female incubates a clutch of 3–4 eggs for 14 days, and the young fledge after a further 19 days.

Voice: Gives a soft, high-pitched, warbling trill from the top of a bush, tree or fence.

Lifespan: Eight years recorded, but up to 16 years in captivity.

Garden needs: Will be attracted to dry seed on a feeding station and to seeding grasses. A regular visitor to garden birdbaths, often arriving during the hottest part of the day.

Similar species: The Yellow Canary is a common garden bird over most of the Karoo and the southern Cape. The familiar cage canary, much loved as a singing house pet, is the domestic form of the Atlantic Canary *Serinus canaria*.

Like most seed-eating birds, the Yellow-fronted Canary must drink regularly and will visit birdbaths after eating.

CAPE CANARY

Serinus canicollis • **13cm**

Although this canary has subtle plumage, the male is noticeably brighter than the female, with a pale ash-grey nape and collar dividing the mustard-yellow face and body. The female has a less well-defined grey wash, with faintly streaked flanks. The male sings sweetly from treetops. Small flocks of up to 20 may be seen feeding on lawns and clearings alongside sparrows and weavers; if disturbed, these canaries call softly as they fly up from the ground to perch in nearby trees, before departing or returning to the ground.

Feeding: The seeds of grasses and a variety of other plants including *Erica*, *Oxalis* and *Eriocephalus* are taken from the seedheads or the ground. Eats the flower buds of Sagewood *Buddleja salviifolia* as well as the seeds of ornamental Lavender *Lavandula spica*. Termites and other small insects are taken when the opportunity arises and are actively sought out for feeding to the young.

Breeding: The breeding cycle usually begins in November, but sometimes as early as September. A small, thick-walled, cup-shaped nest of plant stems is bound to a cross branch with cobwebs, usually on the outer branch of a leafy shrub. The female incubates the clutch of 2–5 eggs for 12–14 days, and the young fledge after a further 17 days.

Voice: Gives a melodious series of rippling, high-pitched warbles, sometimes lasting for up to 15 minutes.

Lifespan: Five years recorded.

Garden needs: Open areas, especially cropped lawns with small, seeding forbs and weeds. Will visit feeding tables for seeds, and birdbaths to drink and bathe.

Similar species: None.

The male Cape Canary is distinguished by his pale grey nape and mantle.

BRIMSTONE CANARY
Crithagra sulphuratus • 15cm

This robust sulphur-yellow bird with its heavy cone-shaped bill is the largest of the southern African canaries. Females are slightly duller than the males. They are frequent visitors to suburban gardens in coastal and mountainous areas around Cape Town, Hermanus and Port Elizabeth, especially where *Protea* and Wild Camphor *Tarchonanthus littoralis* occur. Most often seen in pairs. 'Brimstone' is an obselete word for the flammable mineral sulphur – a reference to the yellow colour of their plumage. Formerly known as the Bully Canary, although it does not make a habit of harassing other birds.

Feeding: Takes large seeds and hard-skinned berries from a wide variety of herbs and shrubs, plucking them directly from the plants or collecting them from the ground. Visits dry protea flower heads to extract the woolly seeds, and is attracted to sunflower plantations.

Breeding: The breeding cycle usually begins in August, sometimes earlier, although breeding has been recorded throughout the year. A cup-shaped nest lined with soft plant down is built within a leafy shrub. The female incubates a clutch of three eggs for 14 days, and the young fledge at around 16 days.

Voice: Gives a sequence of rambling, not particularly melodic, warbles.

Lifespan: Twelve years recorded.

Garden needs: Seeding Wild Camphor is highly attractive to these canaries – they eat the seeds and collect the white down to line their nests. Will be attracted to sunflowers at feeding stations and is a regular visitor to garden birdbaths.

Similar species: The smaller Yellow Canary is a common garden bird over most of the Karoo and the southern Cape.

The Brimstone Canary uses it large bill to crack open strong seeds, including those of proteas.

STREAKY-HEADED SEEDEATER
Crithagra gularis • **15cm**

A rather nondescript member of the canary family, lacking any yellow coloration whatsoever. Its most noteworthy feature is its bold white or pale buff supercilium. Males and females are alike and usually go about in pairs or small flocks during winter. Occurs across the highveld and bushveld, southwards through KwaZulu-Natal and westwards along the Garden Route to the Cape Peninsula. Birds in the southwestern Cape are darker than populations in the north and east. Being unobtrusive, it is easily overlooked or mistaken for a female weaver or sparrow. However, at the onset of the breeding season, males perch conspicuously and sing a distinctive, melodious canary's song.

Feeding: Collects small seeds from grasses and weeds as well as larger *Protea* seeds. Also eats soft petals and the anthers of various flowers and is particularly fond of nectar, visiting flowering *Aloe*, *Erythrina*, *Schotia* and *Tecoma*, among others. Will also eat ripe figs and berries, including those of the invasive *Lantana*, *Morus* and *Opuntia*.

Breeding: The breeding cycle begins in August in the winter-rainfall region, later to the north and east. A small cup-shaped nest is constructed from leaf petioles and other thin plant material and placed in the outer branches of a protea or some other small but leafy tree. The female incubates a clutch of 2–4 eggs for 14 days, and the young fledge at around 17 days.

Voice: A sequence of melodious whistles, chirps and buzzes is usually given from a conspicuous song post.

Lifespan: Ten years recorded.

Garden needs: Seeding grasses will attract this species, as will dry seeds on a feeding station; also comes for apples and other fruit. A regular visitor to garden birdbaths.

The Streaky-headed Seedeater is easily overlooked, or mistaken for a female sparrow, because it lacks bold markings.

Similar species: The Lark-like Bunting may visit gardens in the drier western half of the region, often gathering in large flocks at birdbaths.

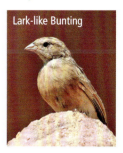

Lark-like Bunting

EXTRAORDINARY AND UNUSUAL GARDEN VISITORS

On the previous pages, the birds most likely to visit suburban gardens in the major towns and cities of southern Africa have been described. Of course, other species may be occasional visitors or show up unexpectedly outside their usual range. Seeing something out of the ordinary, or 'getting a new garden bird', is always exciting. As the old saying goes, 'birds have wings' so there is nothing to stop a bird from turning up almost anywhere.

Habitat specialists, especially open-country species such as larks and cisticolas, are very unlikely to appear in a built-up area. However, some of the most unusual and rarely seen birds have been recorded in gardens, and such birds are actually more likely to be spotted in gardens than in their natural habitat, simply because there are more people around to notice them.

The African Pitta is considered to be the 'holy grail' among local bird-watchers. This multicoloured rarity breeds mostly in the hot Zambezi Valley but may undertake erratic long-distance flights around the subcontinent. Pittas fly after dark, no doubt using the stars for orientation, and can be confused by artificial lights. This is why your chances of finding one in a garden setting are actually higher than of finding one in natural forest or bush – indeed, most South African records are of individuals that were stunned or killed by flying into illuminated windows at night.

Over the years, African Pittas have been recorded in towns such as Potchefstroom, Durban and Port Elizabeth, and the last known record appears to be of a bird seen and photographed in a Barberton garden in 2014. With so few people actually taking notice of birds in their garden, and fewer still recognising anything unusual, the majority of rare birds must go completely undetected.

Among the list of unusual rarities that have been recorded in southern African gardens in the past few years are Collared Flycatcher, Eurasian

How many people would like to see this bird on their washing line? Narina Trogon at Kilmorna Manor, Schoemanskloof, South Africa.

The Green Twinpsot is a reclusive bird, usually confined to forest, but it can be a garden visitor in Nelspruit and towns along the east coast of South Africa.

Blackcap and Spotted Crake, while a Rufous-tailed Scrub Robin took up residence in a public park close to Ottery in the Western Cape in July 2016.

Perhaps the most extraordinary garden bird record in recent years was a Pel's Fishing Owl that appeared in Newlands, Cape Town, in September 2012, where it was discovered feeding on koi and goldfish in ornamental ponds. Quite how this owl got to Cape Town from its usual haunts in northern KwaZulu-Natal, the lowveld, Zimbabwe or northern Botswana remains a mystery.

One rare bird that usually goes unseen in gardens is the Buff-spotted Flufftail. This elusive member of the rail family has a peculiar drawn-out call, reminiscent of a foghorn, which is given at night or on cloudy days. The ghostly sound can be heard over some distance and appears to have ventriloquial properties, which make the calling bird very difficult to locate.

Localised populations of some bird species, such as twinspots or trogons, may inhabit particular suburbs or individual gardens, and parts of Durban and Pietermaritzburg are well-known for their resident Crowned Eagles.

The Pel's Fishing Owl that appeared in Constantia and Newlands in 2012 created huge excitement among Cape Town birders and demonstrated how the unexpected can happen.

For those interested in joining the SA Rare Bird News email group to receive up-to-the-minute information on rarity sightings, email Trevor Hardaker at hardaker@mweb.co.za. Should you happen to locate a rare bird, contact Trevor via email (as above) or at 082 780 0376 as soon as possible so that he can spread the word to other keen birders in the area. If you are able to photograph the bird, you are also encouraged to email your photo to him. The sooner your rare sighting is reported, the better the chance for other birders to have an opportunity to see it.

The White Stinkwood *Celtis africana* puts on a lovely autumn show before dropping its leaves. Groenfontein, Calitzdorp.

THE PLANTS

The plants you select determine which birds will be attracted to your garden. For the greatest diversity of species in a built-up area, it's best to grow mainly indigenous plants, especially those particular to your region.

CHOOSING AND PLACING PLANTS

If your primary goal is to attract birds into your garden, then planting trees, shrubs and climbers that bear berries and fruits should be your top priority. Birds also need cover and sites where they can sing and nest, so the shape and structure of the plants selected will play an important role in the ideal bird garden.

Before choosing plants, take stock of the space you have available. With trees in particular, it is vital to envisage how big a given species will get, and what shape it might be in five, 10 or 20 years' time. Some trees have powerful subsurface roots, some have wide-spreading canopies, and others have dense foliage that can greatly limit the sunlight reaching your house or other plants.

It is a troublesome and costly process to remove a large tree, and you may feel remorse when a plant you have nurtured for several years, but put in the wrong location, has to be felled. When establishing a new garden, it is tempting to include as many of your favourite tree species as possible, but bear in mind the old adage 'less is more'. Unless you have a very large plot, the features and attributes of individual trees can easily be lost when they are crowded together, and roots can also damage walls, drains and driveways.

Other key issues to consider are your climate, aspect and soil (see 'The Climate and biomes of southern Africa', p.11). There are three regions in the country that are quite distinct and impose

The spectacular Guernsey Lily *Nerine sarniensis* is native to the southwestern Cape but can be grown virtually anywhere.

limitations on the trees and plants that will grow there. Firstly, in the highveld and Karoo the winters are cold and dry, and subzero temperatures and heavy frost can occur, which means plants native to the warmer lowveld and coastal regions won't survive here. Secondly, the southwestern Cape receives its rainfall during the cold winter months and the summers are hot and dry, which does not suit some species, although it is surprising to see what can grow in this part of the country. Lastly, the bushveld and lowveld experience summers that may be too hot for temperate plants from the highveld and southern Cape.

Up until the 1980s, few indigenous species were planted in most gardens, simply because commercial nurseries didn't propagate or sell them. Even invasive wattles and pines were sold at nurseries and widely planted. Today, the trend is firmly with indigenous plants, and all good nurseries stock a range of different-sized specimens. While locally indigenous trees (species native to your immediate surroundings) support a web of life and are ecologically preferable, it is very often the case that a garden has various old or sizable non-native species. This is not necessarily a problem – a gnarled old oak tree, for example, is an asset to birds and people alike, and many beautiful trees from other parts of the world make wonderful garden subjects and pose no invasive threat.

However, certain invasive plant species should never be planted in southern Africa, and should be removed from your property if possible, as they pose a great threat to biodiversity (see 'Invasive alien plants', p.181).

PLANT NAMES

In contrast to bird names, many people are familiar with the scientific names of plants, and these are usually preferable because the common names of many species are actually misleading as they allude to relationships that do not exist: the Wild Peach, for example, is in no way related to the peach that we eat, the Buffalo Thorn is not eaten by buffalo, and no amount of Wild Dagga inhalation will get you high (not that this author has tried). On the other hand, some common names are appropriate and deeply entrenched in the language, such that few people refer to trees such as Marula, Mopane and Baobab by their scientific names.

As with bird names, the names of plants sometimes create controversy or unease, so that many people stick to using older, outdated names. In 2011, at a meeting of the International Botanical Congress, the Australian and African acacias were separated (not entirely surprising, as the former have no spines or thorns and are known as wattles), and Australian botanists lobbied successfully to retain the name for their plants, while the thorny African species were placed into the genera *Vachellia* or *Senegalia*.

Paperbark Thorn *Vachelia sieberiana*, Nelspruit

The Skukuza Nursery in the Kruger National Park is a wonderful source of indigenous trees and shrubs.

50 BIRD-FRIENDLY TREES, SHRUBS AND CLIMBERS

This section features 50 indigenous trees, shrubs and creepers with particular appeal for birds. Similar and related species are grouped together. Although it may be tempting to grow as many species as you can, you need to consider the overall appearance that you want to achieve with your garden space. For this reason, an illustration of the general shape and the average height in cultivation of each featured tree or shrub is provided – these are guidelines only and suggest average, not maximum dimensions.

When planting a new tree, always dig a hole that is two or three times wider than the root ball in the bag; although it is not necessary to dig deeper than the depth of the root ball, it is a good idea to loosen the soil below before planting. Once the tree is in position, the hole can be backfilled with a mixture of compost and the excavated soil. Stamp the soil down so that it is slightly lower than the surrounding ground, to allow water to collect there and be retained. The tree should be watered regularly in its first year, but thereafter left to send its roots down to find moisture.

BIGLEAF TREE
Anthocleista grandiflora
Average 15–20m; Deciduous

This tall, open-branched tree is native to the foothills of the escarpment in Mpumalanga and its range extends northwards into the Eastern Highlands of Zimbabwe and tropical Africa. It makes a spectacular addition to a garden in frost-free areas in KwaZulu-Natal, eastern Mpumalanga and Limpopo, where the oval fruits attract turacos, barbets and starlings as well as fruit bats. Its branches are never entirely free of the huge leaves (60cm long) and afford nesting opportunities for goshawks, woodpeckers and barbets. The flowers appear in summer and have a pungent scent to attract pollinating hawkmoths at night.

TASSELBERRY
Antidesma venosum
Average 4m; Deciduous

Few trees produce berries in such abundance; both its Zulu *(umHlalanyoni)* and Afrikaans *(voëlsitboom)* common names refer to the fact that birds relish the annual crop. These small trees bear fruit in autumn (March–May), but since there are separate male and female plants, you'll need a few specimens to ensure that cross-pollination occurs. The droves of white-eyes, bulbuls, thrushes and others that visit may not be able to strip the bounty, and heaps of fallen berries may pile up below the tree. A rich insect fauna usually lives in the tree, making it a productive foraging site for warblers, apalises and flycatchers. Will only grow in the frost-free eastern parts of southern Africa.

COMMON CABBAGE TREE
Cussonia spicata
Average 8–12m; Deciduous

Tall lollipop-shaped tree native to the foothills of the escarpment in Mpumalanga, KwaZulu-Natal and eastern Zimbabwe. It is widely cultivated in Gauteng, although young plants are susceptible to frost here, so the hardier *C. paniculata* is more appropriate. It is fast-growing, takes up very little space and looks best in a grove of three or more. The straight trunk can provide an ideal site for the placement of a nest box or log, and woodpeckers and barbets can easily excavate the soft wood of older trees. The small fruits are borne on spikes and sought out by many birds.

PAPERBARK THORN
Vachellia (Acacia) sieberiana
Average 6–8m; Partly deciduous

Native to the foothills of the eastern escarpment but able to tolerate frost, this umbrella-shaped tree is grown successfully throughout most of Gauteng, the southwestern Cape and the Garden Route. Fast-growing if it receives plenty of water, the Paperbark Thorn is very attractive to ants, aphids, beetles and bugs, so insectivorous birds constantly explore its bark, branches and foliage. Green Wood-hoopoes regularly forage in this tree, as the ragged papery bark provides shelter for spiders, geckos, skinks and centipedes. Several bird species like to build their nests in the tangle of thorns below the tree's crown.

FEVER TREE
Vachellia (Acacia) xanthophloea
Average 15–20m; Partly deciduous

This is one of the fastest-growing indigenous trees and increasingly popular as an ornamental garden subject, looking particularly impressive if two or three are grown together in a grove on a large lawn. Native to northern KwaZulu-Natal and the floodplains of the Kruger, it does surprisingly well in other parts of southern Africa, even in the southern Cape with its winter rainfall. As is typical of thorn trees, it attracts large numbers of ants and other insects, so insectivorous birds find plenty to eat. Weavers prefer this tree above all others for nesting, and sparrows like to wedge their scruffy nests among the thorns.

SWEET THORN
Vachellia (Acacia) karroo
Average 3–6m; Deciduous

The most widespread of the native 'acacias' and a fast-growing tree for a new garden. Able to grow in clay or sandy soil, and frost-hardy. Will form an attractive rounded shape if standing alone, but also forms a good screen or thicket when grown alongside other trees and shrubs. The tangled thorny branches provide ideal nesting sites for smaller birds. A mass of ball-shaped golden flowers appears in midsummer, attracting bees, butterflies and many other small insects.

FLATCROWN
Albizia adianthifolia
Average 15–18m; Deciduous

This low-branching tree takes on an umbrella shape with an expansive crown and provides marvellous summer shade in a large garden. The open branches provide foraging opportunities for wood-hoopoes and woodpeckers, while sunbirds feed on the nectar and canaries nibble on the anthers and petals. When dry, the seed pods harbour beetle larvae, which are sought out by birds such as the Cardinal Woodpecker, Black-backed Puffback, Southern Black Tit and Long-billed Crombec. Native to northern KwaZulu-Natal and eastern Zimbabwe, but grows well in the frost-free eastern parts of southern Africa.

LARGELEAF ALBIZIA
Albizia versicolor
Average 6–8m; Deciduous

An elegant, open-branched tree found in sandy soils on the lower slopes of hillsides or in undulating bushveld, quite often along streams or riverbanks. Native to the northeastern parts of South Africa as well as much of Zimbabwe and northern Botswana. The flowers have long white stamens tipped with lime-green, and appear in October among the fresh new foliage. These flowers attract hordes of insects, so insectivorous birds frequently inhabit the tree. One of the most beautiful indigenous trees, but not often cultivated, it requires little water but is frost-sensitive so cannot survive on the highveld.

SACRED CORAL TREE
Erythrina lysistemon
Average 5–10m; Deciduous

A low-spreading, fast-growing tree that attracts birds throughout the year. Native to the foothills of the eastern escarpment and northern bushveld, as well as Zimbabwe, but can be cultivated in any area without severe frost, including parts of Johannesburg and the winter-rainfall region of the southern Cape. August is the peak flowering month, with glorious scarlet blooms appearing on the naked branches. Sunbirds find the flowers irresistible, as do Cape White-eyes, Cape Glossy Starlings and Black-headed Orioles. The wood is soft, so barbets frequently select a large branch in which to excavate a nest hole.

COASTAL CORAL TREE
Erythrina caffra
Average 5–10m; Deciduous

Very similar to the previous species, being native to the coastal areas of KwaZulu-Natal and the Eastern Cape, but commonly cultivated right along the southern coast to the Cape Peninsula. Does not do well inland, where *E. lysistemon* fares better and is recommended. Both are spectacular trees that can form a focal point in any garden, but never planted too close to a house or wall as the subsurface roots are expansive. August is the peak flowering month, with sunbirds and other nectar-feeders visiting the mass of scarlet blooms.

WEEPING BOERBEAN
Schotia brachypetala
Average 4–8m; Partly deciduous

A medium-sized, spreading tree native to bushveld habitat in northern KwaZulu-Natal and to the lowveld, as well as Zimbabwe, but able to tolerate varied climatic conditions – it is successfully cultivated in Johannesburg and even the southern Cape. In full bloom, no other tree attracts as many birds: regular patrons include nectar-seeking sunbirds, starlings, parrots, drongos, orioles, weavers, canaries and white-eyes. Within this tree's natural range small beetles parasitise the woody seed pods, and tits and woodpeckers seek out their larvae.

WHITE STINKWOOD
Celtis africana

Average 15–18m; Deciduous

Under optimum conditions this is a tall, open-branched, fast-growing tree. It can withstand frost and is a good choice for a small garden, as its bare winter branches allow sunlight into homes, while the leafy summer boughs provide shade. Thick-billed Weavers relish the hard-skinned berries, while the clusters of creamy-white flowers attract many insects that provide food for white-eyes, batises and flycatchers. Outer branches provide suitable nesting sites for the African Paradise Flycatcher, while the Red-chested Cuckoo may claim the canopy as a call site.

PIGEONWOOD
Trema orientalis

Average 5–10m; Semi-deciduous

A slender, fast-growing, pioneer tree of temperate forest. Does well in full sun and can provide quick cover and shade in developing gardens. A good choice for a smaller garden. Young trees tend to have a rather lax and wobbly shape, so it is advisable to create a small grove of three or more specimens that will mature into a mini forest. Hundreds of tiny black berries appear in late summer and are relished by pigeons as well as greenbuls, mousebirds and tinkerbirds. Cuckoos feed on the caterpillars of Wahlberg's Emperor Moth, which are attracted to the leaves.

CAPE ASH
Ekebergia capensis

Average 12–15m; Semi-deciduous

Tall, bushy tree native to forests and riverine strips from the Eastern Cape into the lowveld and north into Zimbabwe; fast-growing and a good starter tree for the indigenous gardener. It fares well in the winter-rainfall region, and it is widely grown in Cape Town and other parts of the southern Cape. The large berries ripen to a bright pink colour and are relished by mousebirds, bulbuls, barbets, hornbills, turacos and others. This tree is most attractive in a dry autumn when its foliage turns from yellow to bright red.

WILD PEACH
Kiggelaria africana
Average 4–6m; Semi-deciduous

A small fast-growing tree or bushy shrub native to temperate forest edges from the Cape Peninsula to the foothills of the northern Drakensberg; also occurs along streams and on the cooler southern sides of rocky outcrops across the highveld. The marble-sized fruits split open into a star shape, presenting the wax-coated orange seeds to frugivorous birds. A common butterfly, the Garden Acraea *Acraea horta*, lays its eggs on the leaves and the resultant browsing caterpillars can occur in great abundance, which attracts Red-chested, Diederik and other cuckoos. Thrives in Johannesburg, Pretoria, Bloemfontein, Durban and Cape Town and should be included in any indigenous garden aimed at attracting birds.

WILD PLUM
Harpephyllum caffrum
Average 6–10m; Evergreen, but old and new leaves are bright red

A large, open-branched tree that can eventually form an expansive crown if given enough space. With its attractive dense foliage it also forms a good screen or barrier. Native to warmer coastal regions and escarpment forests, but able to withstand slight frost and can do well in highveld gardens if given a warm, sheltered position. The orange-coloured plums are beloved by turacos, mousebirds and other frugivores.

WILD PEAR
Dombeya rotundifolia
Average 3–5m; Deciduous

Common across much of the northern and eastern parts of southern Africa, this is a good tree for smaller gardens, where it should be placed in a sunny north-facing position. Able to tolerate a wide range of conditions and can be successfully cultivated in the winter-rainfall regions of the southern Cape. One of the first trees to flower in early spring, its papery white blooms make a very attractive show. Although the wild pear does not provide fruit, seeds or nectar to birds, the many invertebrates that feed on its leaves, pollinate the flowers and hide in its fissured bark are attractive to insectivores.

RIVER BUSHWILLOW
Combretum erythrophyllum
Average 4–8m; Deciduous

An open-branched tree that usually takes on a crooked but attractive form, with the low outer branches sometimes touching the ground. One of numerous *Combretum* species in southern Africa, but the most tolerant of varied climatic conditions. Native to riverbanks and drainage lines in the highveld and lowveld, it is relatively fast-growing and can withstand the harshest frosts. For birds, it provides perching sites, shelter, roosts and nesting sites, while the catkin flowers attract many small insects.

FLAME CREEPER
Combretum microphyllum
Scrambles up to 20m; Partly deciduous

A vigorous scrambler that can cover fences and pergolas, putting on metres of growth in a year. Masses of tiny scarlet flowers appear in spring, turning the entire plant bright red and attracting sunbirds and canaries, among others. If allowed to scramble into a tree, it may eventually take over, so some judicious pruning will be required. Native to riverine thickets in the warmer parts of South Africa and Zimbabwe, making it a wonderful plant for lowveld and coastal gardens.

PRIDE OF DE KAAP
Bauhinia galpinii
Scrambles up to 15m; Evergreen

Not strictly a tree, this woody climber winds its way up into other vegetation. Native to the warmer northeastern parts of South Africa as well as much of Zimbabwe, but hardy and widely cultivated, even in the southern Cape. Its  instinct is to scramble into and over other plants, but it can be clipped into a neat and tidy bush. Although not rich in nectar, its showy coral-red flowers attract butterflies, while the tangled stems and branches provide roosting and nesting sites for various birds.

CAMPHOR TREE
Tarchonanthus littoralis
Average 3–5m; Evergreen

A bushy shrub or small tree found in coastal districts from the Cape Peninsula to the Eastern Cape and KwaZulu-Natal. Tolerant of sea spray and wind, it can form an excellent screen along a garden border. For inland gardens, the almost indistinguishable *T. camphoratus*, which occurs on rocky slopes in the highveld and Drakensberg, is more suitable. The Camphor Tree's greatest appeal for birds is its fluffy seedheads, which appear on the crown in late winter and provide ideal material for nest lining.

SAGEWOOD
Buddleja salviifolia
Average 2–4m; Evergreen

A sprawling lax-stemmed shrub with a wide distribution, occurring naturally along drainage lines and in rocky kloofs as well as on forest edges. Fast-growing, the plant begins to bud in July, producing dense spikes of tiny lilac flowers that perfume the evening air. Butterflies, bees and small wasps visit the flowers and attract flycatchers and the like. Can be clipped into a neat shape, but best planted on the border of a garden where it can form a tangle suitable for bird roosts.

JACKET PLUM
Pappea capensis
Average 4–6m; Semi-deciduous

A slow-growing tree that develops a tangled crown of stiff branchlets and takes on a gnarled appearance. Occurs around rocky outcrops and is able to tolerate frost and drought. A variety of wasps, flies, beetles, butterflies, moths and bees attend the strongly scented flowers, attracting flycatchers among others. The small jelly-coated berries contained in velvety-green capsules ('jackets') are never on the tree for long, as they are greedily consumed by white-eyes, bulbuls, barbets, starlings and thrushes.

TREE FUCHSIA
Halleria lucida
Average 2–5m; Evergreen

Because it flowers and fruits for up to eight months, this is a superb plant to have in any garden. Although it is a sprawling, unshapely shrub, with frequent clipping it can be turned into a hedge or allowed to form a small tree. Native to the highveld, eastern escarpment and south coast, including the Cape Peninsula, it is easily cultivated throughout the country. From May to February it bears a profusion of tubular orange flowers, which attract sunbirds and white-eyes. The small berries are relished by bulbuls, starlings and others.

BUSH TICKBERRY
Chrysanthemoides monilifera
Average 2–3m; Evergreen

This bushy shrub or small tree is native to coastal plains and mountainous areas from the Cape to Limpopo. A pioneer plant, it grows rapidly and produces a profusion of yellow daisy flowers followed by small berries that are irresistible to birds such as bulbuls, mousebirds, Cape Spurfowl and African Olive Pigeon. An ideal starter plant for a winter-rainfall garden. This is a declared weed in Australia where it suffocates local flora, in the same way that Australian wattles do here in southern Africa.

WHITE MILKWOOD
Sideroxylon inerme
Average 3–8m; Evergreen

A dense, glossy-leaved shrub or gnarled tree of coastal districts from the Cape Peninsula to northern KwaZulu-Natal. Slow-growing but perfect as a windbreak or feature plant. The masses of small greenish flowers have a pungent tangy odour that attracts swarms of small flies, which sip the nectar and pollinate the tree. Swallows, martins and swifts circle, scooping up the winged insects with bills agape. Bulbuls, starlings and barbets also feed on the clusters of large red to purple berries.

WATERBERRY
Syzygium cordatum
Average 5–10m; Evergreen

This dense tree has bluish-green foliage. It is native to the Eastern Cape and extends northwards into the lowveld and bushveld, as well as throughout much of Zimbabwe and northern Botswana, where it occurs along riverbanks and on rocky outcrops. Fast-growing, hardy and adaptable, it also does well outside of its natural range – in Cape Town, the southern Cape and Gauteng. The rough bark provides hideaways for invertebrates, so wood-hoopoes frequently inspect the trunk and branches. The large berries ripen to a deep purple and are fed upon by many birds.

BIG NUMNUM
Carissa macrocarpa
Average 2–4m; Evergreen

This spiny, glossy-leaved shrub is native to the warm coastal strip from the Eastern Cape to northern KwaZulu-Natal, but is able to withstand most conditions and is frequently planted as a screen or clipped hedge in gardens across the region. Grows rapidly if placed in a warm sunny position. Moths and butterflies pollinate the sweetly scented white flowers, and both frugivores and humans relish the large oval berries, which ripen to a scarlet colour.

BUFFALO THORN
Ziziphus mucronata
Average 3–6m; Partly deciduous

Armed with formidable thorns, this glossy-leaved small tree occurs over most of southern Africa, except in the winter-rainfall regions of the Cape. It makes a perfect barrier and is tolerant of drought and frost, so is an ideal choice in areas where more sensitive plants struggle. Insectivores such as robin-chats, shrikes and warblers find plenty to eat and like to nest within its protective branches. The Grey Go-away-bird relishes its dry-textured berries. Because it is thorny, it is best planted at the edge of a garden.

BROOM CLUSTER FIG
Ficus sur
Average 4–8m; Deciduous

This is the most widespread of our many native fig species and an ideal choice for most gardens, as it never reaches the massive proportions of other fig trees. Bears the biggest figs of any local *Ficus*. The juicy pink figs occur in large hanging clusters on the trunk or lower branches and attract droves of bulbuls, starlings, barbets, white-eyes and other frugivores, as well as many insects, including the fig wasps that pollinate this tree. Deserving of a prominent position in any garden.

NATAL STRANGLER FIG
Ficus natalensis
Average 8–12m; Partly deciduous or evergreen

Native to KwaZulu-Natal and eastern Zimbabwe, but does well and grows rapidly all along the coastal strip as far south as the Cape Peninsula. A full-sized Natal Strangler Fig is impressive, with a spreading canopy much wider than the tree is high. Provides dense summer shade but is really suitable only for larger gardens, where it becomes a focal point. The small orange figs are a magnet for white-eyes, starlings and other birds.

NATAL MAHOGANY
Trichilia emetica
Average 10–12m; Evergreen

This large tree with dense foliage is found along lowveld rivers and in coastal Zululand, as well as in Zimbabwe and northern Botswana. It does not thrive far outside of its natural range, but is a very popular garden and roadside tree in places such as Harare, Nelspruit and Durban. Few trees provide such dense shade, and ferns and clivias can be grown at its base. For birds, the orange-and-black seeds are a big attraction, while owls like to roost in its dense shade by day.

BROWN IVORY
Berchemia discolor
Average 4–6m; Deciduous

Also known as the Bird Plum, this shapely tree produces an annual crop of small juicy berries that are irresistible to birds, especially starlings, barbets, bulbuls, thrushes and turacos. Native to the warm lowveld and northern KwaZulu-Natal, as well as Zimbabwe, Botswana and northern Namibia, it can be cultivated in Durban or Pretoria but not in the winter-rainfall region or in areas prone to frost. Makes a fine upright specimen in a medium-sized or large garden.

WHITE PEAR
Apodytes dimidiata
Average 3–5m; Evergreen

With its glossy foliage and upright shape, this is a good choice for smaller gardens. Nothing about this plant is reminiscent of a pear tree, so its name is something of a mystery. Native to temperate forests and thickets, it occurs patchily over the eastern parts of the region and grows well in all coastal areas as well as Gauteng, although young plants need to be protected from severe frosts. The profusion of small greenish-white flowers give rise to black berries, each with a fleshy red appendage that attracts bulbuls, starlings and other fruit-eating birds.

PUZZLEBUSH
Ehretia rigida
Average 2–3m; Deciduous

This shrub lacks pretty flowers or fine foliage, but its tangled growth form provides a perfect retreat for smaller birds. If grown in the corner of your garden, its rigid branches will provide a thicket that no cat can penetrate. The small flowers attract butterflies and moths, while the red berries are taken by the Brimstone Canary among others. It is drought and frost resistant. Known in Afrikaans as the *Deurmekaarbos*.

MITZEERIE
Bridelia micrantha
Average 8–12m; Dediduous

A medium-sized, fast-growing tree native to the warm lowveld, the KwaZulu-Natal coast and eastern Zimbabwe, but it may grow in north-facing Gauteng gardens provided it gets enough water and is protected from frost for its first two years. In its natural range it often grows close to water and can survive regular waterlogging. In autumn its foliage turns beautiful shades of amber and rust. The small berries are taken by white-eyes and other frugivores.

CAPE HONEYSUCKLE
Tecoma (Tecomaria) capensis
Average 2–4m; Semi-deciduous

This scrambler will crawl into other shrubs and bushes if not regularly pruned. Fast-growing, it roots from pendulous branchlets, forming a thicket. Occurs along the coast from Hermanus to northern KwaZulu-Natal and

inland through the lowveld. It is able to withstand frost and is one of the most widely cultivated native plants in southern Africa. The tubular flowers attract sunbirds throughout summer; best grown in full sun.

KEURBOOM
Virgilia oroboides
Average 6–8m; Semi-deciduous

Native to the southern Cape, this is a slender, fast-growing pioneer tree of temperate forests that does well in full sun and can provide quick cover and shade in developing gardens. The canopy is sparse, allowing plenty of light to reach plants below. Does not have a long life, however, usually dying at about 12 years, but saplings will have begun to grow below it by then. In the bird garden, its main benefit is providing structure and form. The lilac flowers are visited by large nectar-seeking carpenter bees.

POTATO BUSH
Phyllanthus reticulatus
Scrambles up to 8m; Semi-deciduous

A scrambler that reaches into larger trees, but can be clipped into a small bush. Native to the lowveld and the KwaZulu-Natal coast, as well as Zimbabwe and northern Botswana. It occurs along rivers or in thickets around termite mounds. From June to August it produces small, waxy green flowers that release a delicious baked potato scent and, for those who enjoy this, it is reason enough to cultivate the plant. The small aniseed-sized berries are deep purple when ripe and are relished by bulbuls, thrushes, barbets and starlings.

KAREE
Searsia (Rhus) lancea
Averages 3–5m; Evergreen

A medium-sized, open-branched tree that often assumes an interesting shape, with graceful arching branches. Occurs over much of South Africa, as well as southeastern Botswana and central Namibia, but is absent from the southwestern Cape and the warm lowveld. However, it can be grown virtually anywhere. Fast-growing and able to withstand extreme frost and drought, its main appeal for birds is as a structure for nesting and perching.

DUNE CROWBERRY
Searsia (Rhus) crenata
Average 2–4m; Evergreen

This is a compact, dense shrub able to withstand sea spray and strong winds. It forms a neat hedge if clipped and is thus a perfect nesting place for mousebirds and others. The small berries appear in profusion during winter and feed multitudes of bulbuls, white-eyes and many more. The foliage is attractive and has a spicy scent when broken or clipped.

CAPE BEECH
Rapanea melanophloeos
Average 4–8m; Evergreen

This hardy tree occurs in coastal thickets and on forest edges from the Cape to eastern Zimbabwe and is able to tolerate cold and windy conditions. It is a good choice for creating a garden thicket or grove, and its dense canopy provides deep shade. The flowers are insignificant, but small berries are produced in profusion and attract barbets, bulbuls and white-eyes. Tends to sucker, so should not be planted too close to a driveway or wall.

CAPE HOLLY
Ilex mitis
Average 3–5m; Evergreen

A dense shrub or small tree native to higher-rainfall regions from the southern Cape to the Drakensberg escarpment, as well as sheltered kloofs on the highveld and in eastern Zimbabwe. Can grow quite rapidly in Gauteng and Cape gardens if given a sheltered spot with plenty of water. Produces a large crop of scarlet berries in autumn and attracts a steady flow of frugivorous birds. Older trees have rough bark that harbours invertebrates, which will appeal to insectivorous birds.

CHEESEWOOD
Pittosporum viridiflorum
Average 3–5m; Evergreen

This is a wide-ranging plant occurring throughout southern Africa, except for the semi-arid west and hot lowveld valleys. With its dense glossy foliage it makes an excellent screen, but can also be clipped and shaped into a small tree. Happy in coastal areas as well as on the highveld plateau, it grows quite quickly if well watered. Birds such as bulbuls, mousebirds and pigeons relish the glossy orange berries.

WILD DAGGA
Leonotis leonurus
Average 1–2m; Partly deciduous

This plant usually has a straggly shape, but it responds well to pruning and can be clipped into a tight bush. This and several closely related species occur naturally over most of southern Africa. Its numerous upright stems bear distinctive ball-shaped clusters of orange flowers, and the leaves are lance-shaped, with toothed margins. Flowering can last for several months, attracting a steady stream of sunbirds and other nectarivores, and the dried flower heads remain on the plant for a long time.

WILD BANANA
Strelitzia nicolai
Average 6–8m; Evergreen

With their huge strappy leaves, Strelitzias have a tropical look and make excellent feature plants. The extravagant waxy flowers drip with nectar, which continually attracts sunbirds, orioles, starlings and white-eyes. The Wild Banana is a fast-growing plant in most situations but, as it can't cope with frost or drought, it is only suitable for well-watered coastal and lowveld gardens. The smaller, orange-flowered *Strelitzia regina* is a better option for smaller gardens.

WILD LABURNUM
Calpurnia aurea
Average 4–6m; Deciduous or evergreen

This is a slender, fast-growing tree ideal for smaller gardens. Although the flowers and seed pods are not utilised by birds, it has attractive fern-like foliage and will provide structure and shade to a new garden. Grows naturally in the eastern half of southern Africa, but adapts well to the winter-rainfall region of the southern Cape. The showy bunches of bright yellow flowers are pollinated by carpenter bees.

SUGARBUSH
Protea repens
Average 3–4m; Evergreen

This small shrub or thickset tree has flower heads that vary in colour from creamy-white to deep red. Occurs on mountain slopes and flats in the winter-rainfall area from the southwestern Cape to Grahamstown. Although not the most spectacular of the proteas, it is the most reliable and adaptable in cultivation, being able to tolerate sandy or clay soils. The nectar-rich flowers are visited by sunbirds, sugarbirds and weavers as well as bees and other insects.

STINK-LEAF SUGARBUSH
Protea susannae
Average 3–4m; Evergreen

A compact, robust shrub native to the Overberg region of the southwestern Cape, but one of the easiest proteas to grow throughout the winter-rainfall region, as it can cope with acid or alkaline soils. Showy pink flowers appear from April to August, brightening up the winter garden; in recent years a variety of cultivars have been created, including the popular 'Pink Ice' (pictured here). The common name comes from the sulphurous smell given off by crushed leaves.

PINCUSHION
Leucospermum cordifolium
Average 2m; Evergreen

A bushy shrub with a single main stem and horizontally spreading branches that create a rounded shape. Occurs naturally only in the winter-rainfall region of the Cape, in acidic, nutrient-poor soils. The spectacular flower heads appear from July to November, attracting sugarbirds and sunbirds as well as small scarab beetles that act as pollinators. Leaves are oblong and face upwards on the branches in a scale-like manner. In recent years a number of hybrids and cultivars have been developed and these are available at many nurseries.

PROTEAS AND OTHER FYNBOS PLANTS

The winter-rainfall region of the southern and southwestern Cape is home to a mind-boggling diversity of plants – over 7,000 species – most of which are found nowhere else on Earth. These plants are adapted to the climate, soil and bushfire cycle unique to the fynbos biome. Many species are further restricted to a small range within this biome.

Growing fynbos plants outside their restricted natural range can be a challenge, but hugely rewarding. The best approach is to select proteas and other species that occur naturally close to where you live, so explore the closest hillside or nature trail and walk around your neighbourhood.

Most proteas and ericas grow in coarse, well-drained, acidic soil and do not like fertilisers rich in phosphorus or potassium. Creating a natural fynbos garden requires some trial and error, but is well worth the effort, as these splendid plants produce nectar and host invertebrates highly attractive to birds.

In addition to the woody proteas and ericas, fynbos also supports an astonishing variety of bulbous plants, including many spectacular species of *Watsonia*, *Gladiolus*, *Brunsvigia* and *Nerine* that are easy to grow in gardens. Also characteristic of the fynbos biome are the so-called 'Cape Reeds' – the grass-like restios with their graceful forms and coppery flower heads or bracts; these attractive plants are becoming increasingly popular with gardeners.

An important consideration when gardening with ericas and other fynbos species is never to disturb the soil around their roots; weeds should be cut back rather than pulled out. A mulch of bark and fallen leaves will limit weed growth and preserve soil moisture.

Three spectacular fynbos plants: King Protea *Protea cynaroides*, Prince-of-Wales Heath *Erica perspicua*, and Marsh Pagoda *Mimetes hirtus*

ALOES

Of the many plants in southern Africa, aloes are arguably the most rewarding for the bird gardener and, once established, require little if any attention. Aloes typically have flat succulent leaves arranged in a rosette pattern and vary in size from massive tree aloes, with their thick fibrous trunks, to tiny ground-hugging miniatures. In most species the tubular red, orange or yellow flowers appear in midwinter, massed on spikes that may be singular or branched. Aloes belong to the family Asphodelaceae, which includes the red-hot pokers and bulbines. The exotic Sisal *Agave sisalina* and its relatives are often mistaken for aloes, since they have a similar arrangement of succulent leaves, but the huge green-and-white inflorescences of these Mexican plants (which typically die after flowering) are quite distinctive.

Because they require so little attention and put on such an impressive flowering display, aloes are popular garden subjects in many towns. In addition to providing a blast of colour when it is most appreciated, aloes produce sweet and abundant nectar that attracts a host of birds. Iridescent sunbirds are the most frequent visitors to aloe flowers, but starlings, orioles, white-eyes, bulbuls, weavers and others also partake of the sugary feast. The flowers attract hordes of insects, especially bees, wasps and ants, which form the basis for other natural food chains.

Although some aloes can tolerate partial shade, most thrive in full sun. They prefer well-drained sandy soils and are thus ideal for sloping gardens. Aloes are easily transplanted, but it is, of course, illegal to take them from the wild. Some gardeners do not seem to like these succulent plants, however, and it is not uncommon to see broken plants piled up on roadsides along with other garden cuttings awaiting collection by the council; such discarded plants are ripe for rescue and will reward you in no time when the first sunbirds arrive to feed on their nectar. When transplanting aloes with damaged roots, it is advisable to let their roots or stumps dry out before planting to reduce the risk of fungal attack.

In recent years, horticulturalists have created a range of 'improved' hybrid cultivar aloes with larger flowers and more vigorous growth, but although these put on an impressive flowering show, they are not favoured by the purists.

The Dune Aloe *Aloe thraskii* is a large and very impressive plant that does best in coastal regions.

The bill of this male Scarlet-chested Sunbird fits perfectly into the tubular flower of this Swazi Aloe *Aloe chabaudii*.

TOP 10 ALOES TO ATTRACT BIRDS:

- Krantz Aloe – *Aloe arborescens*
- Cattail Aloe – *Aloe castanea*
- Swazi Aloe – *Aloe chabaudii*
- Bitter Aloe – *Aloe ferox*
- Spear Aloe – *Aloe lutescens*
- Coral Aloe – *Aloe striata*
- Dune Aloe – *Aloe thraskii*
- Mountain Aloe – *Aloe marlothii*
- French Aloe – *Aloe pluridens*
- Bottlebrush Aloe – *Aloe rupestris*

The Krantz Aloe *Aloe arborescens* is very easy to grow and brings colour, glow and warmth to the winter garden.

This Cape Glossy Starling has become so dusted with the pollen of Mountain Aloe *Aloe marlothii* that its identity might confuse a beginner birder.

DECORATIVE PLANTS

To create attractive flowerbeds, borders or mini-meadows, there is a huge variety of indigenous plants to choose from, but there is obviously no space in this book to describe such a wealth of flora in any detail. Many of these smaller plants may have no direct appeal for birds, but they will play an ecological role by hosting bees and other invertebrates as well as providing colour and interest to your garden. Such plantings are more eco-friendly and require less maintenance than lawn. As with trees, it is best to grow the species that occur naturally around you, but there is no harm in planting a selection of beautiful plants from other parts of the region if they can thrive in your climate. Take a look at what is growing in other gardens around you, or talk to your local nursery for advice.

The various species of *Plectranthus* are fast-growing and require little attention, quickly filling up shady spots and doing particularly well in damper, south-facing situations. In late summer and autumn, they burst into flower, creating a splendid show and a feast for nectar-feeding bees. These plants are very easy to propagate from cuttings; some species are tall shrubs, others ground covers.

The Ribbonbush *Hypoestes aristata* is an evergreen shrub that produces masses of lilac-purple flowers in winter. It favours full sun, grows well across the whole region, and is easily cultivated from cuttings or seeds. The flowers attract pollinating bees and other winged insects, which in turn lure flycatchers. Its main value in the garden is to occupy areas of poor or shallow soil and provide colour in early winter. To prevent the Ribbonbush from becoming straggly and weak, it should be cut right back after flowering.

The Bush Lily *Clivia miniata* is one of the most beautiful and best-loved garden plants. These evergreen lilies are native to the cool shady forests of the eastern parts of the region, but they are surprisingly hardy and flourish in gardens from Cape Town to Johannesburg and Harare, if given sufficient shade (seeing these lilies struggle when planted in full sun is a sad sight as their strap-like leaves are quickly burned). Clivias have swollen tuberous roots and do not require a lot of water, but grow more vigorously when it is available. Over most of the region peak flowering is in September.

Agapanthus are hardy, drought- and frost-resistant lilies, able to grow throughout most of the region, and are familiar to almost everyone. They put on a spectacular midsummer show of cobalt-blue flower heads and are best grown on borders or in clumps. Hybrids are available with flowers in every shade from dark blue to white. The flowers are pollinated by bees and other winged insects. Agapanthus are easily transplanted and can be used to cover exposed areas or prevent soil erosion on slopes.

Ribbonbush *Hypoestes aristata*

Bush Lily *Clivia miniata*

Agapanthus *Agapanthus praecox*

GRASSES

Grasses occur throughout the world and are the foundation for food pyramids that support termites and grasshoppers as well as wildebeest and lions. Humans, too, are dependent on grasses, including wheat, rice and maize. In the garden, grasses are most often grown as lawns, but clumps of uncut grass can be useful 'fillers' that can bind soil to prevent erosion, occupy shady areas and, of course, attract seed-eating birds. In nature, grass growth is stimulated and controlled by grazing herbivores and by fire, neither of which is likely in your garden. To keep the plants vigorous, you should cut them back, but not before they have flowered and set seed in late summer or autumn. Some nurseries sell indigenous grasses, but it is quite easy to cultivate them yourself from seed or by transplanting uprooted plants, in which case the plants should be cut back so that they can resprout.

The Broad-leaved Bristle Grass *Setaria megaphylla* (above) is a robust, tuft-forming plant with pleated leaves that likes semi-shaded areas below tree canopies. Within its range, the Blue Waxbill (top) is one of many seedeaters likely to visit a grass patch in the garden.

INVASIVE ALIEN PLANTS

As mankind has moved products and supplies around the globe, so certain animal and plant species have become established outside of their natural range. If these organisms are able to reproduce and proliferate, they are deemed 'feral' or 'invasive' and, without the ecological constraints (such as parasites and predators) of the land in which they evolved, they can out-compete native species. In recent decades, there has been an explosion of invasive species around the world and many countries devote vast sums of money in attempts to control them, as they threaten biodiversity in general.

All plants produce seeds and each plant species has evolved a particular strategy for the transportation of its seeds so that it may germinate and grow in other places. Some plants have their seeds dispersed by wind, or in other ways such as by snagging in the fur of animals, but a great many produce berries or fruit to tempt an army of seed distributors. Many trees and shrubs produce large quantities of sweet and juicy packages – usually red, orange or purple in colour – that are irresistible to birds, which inadvertently transport and deposit the seeds in their droppings. In this way, bulbuls, mousebirds, pigeons and starlings are responsible for the spread of many troublesome invader plants in southern Africa. The ecologically-minded bird-gardener should not only eradicate any invasive plant species from their property, but also encourage their neighbours and local municipality to do the same.

The yellow berries of the Syringa *Melia azederach* are relished by Grey Go-away-birds, which have probably facilitated the rampant spread of this Indian tree in South Africa.

Bulbuls and mousebirds eat the fleshy red aril of Red-eye Wattle *Acacia cyclops* and consume or carry off the black seeds while feeding.

SOME INVASIVE PLANTS SPREAD BY BIRDS – TO BE REMOVED WHEREVER POSSIBLE

- Australian Myrtle – *Leptospermum laevigatum*
- Bramble – *Rubus* spp.
- Brazilian Pepper Tree – *Schinus terebinthifolius*
- Bugweed – *Solanum mauritianum*
- Cotoneaster – *Cotoneaster* spp.
- Passion Fruits – *Passiflora* spp.
- Guava – *Psidium guajava*
- Firethorn – *Pyracantha* spp.
- Jambolan – *Syzygium cumini*
- Lantana – *Lantana camara*
- Loquat – *Eriobotrya japonica*
- Mulberry – *Morus* spp.
- Potato Creeper – *Solanum seaforthianum*
- Prickly Pear – *Opuntia robusta*
- Privet – *Ligustrum* spp.
- Red-eye Wattle – *Acacia cyclops*
- Syringa – *Melia azedarach*

If you are not familiar with these plants, a quick internet search will enable you to identify them.

BIRDS IN BOTANICAL GARDENS

South Africa has a network of 10 national botanical gardens situated in seven of the nine provinces, while Zimbabwe, Namibia and Botswana each have a single national botanical garden. In all cases, these gardens combine natural vegetation with cultivated plants and formally laid-out sections, together conserving thousands of hectares of biodiversity. The main role of each garden is to allow public access to the botanical splendours of their region and, indeed, over 1.5 million people visit the South African gardens each year. The gardens are important from a plant conservation perspective, with many rare and endangered plant species within the collections. In addition to these state-run gardens, there are many smaller provincial or privately owned gardens in southern Africa.

Visiting these public gardens, some of which are described in what follows, is a marvellous way to get inspiration and information for your own garden, and most have nurseries where plants can be bought. They are also excellent places for bird-watching, and are well worth visiting for the birds alone.

Kirstenbosch National Botanical Garden, Western Cape

One of the world's most celebrated gardens, Kirstenbosch is situated on the eastern slopes of Table Mountain on the Cape Peninsula. Kirstenbosch has an enormous collection of fynbos plants as well as an extraordinary diversity of other African plants. Among the noteworthy birds found here are Cape Sugarbird, Cape Siskin, Orange-breasted Sunbird, Malachite Sunbird, African Grassbird and Cape Batis, and resident Spotted Eagle-Owls often raise their young close to the garden's entrance. Lemon Dove and African Wood Owl live in the forested kloofs.

Kirstenbosch National Botanical Garden

Lowveld National Botanical Garden

Lowveld National Botanical Garden, Mpumalanga

Set on the banks of the Crocodile River in Nelspruit, this verdant paradise has specimens of most of the characteristic bushveld trees as well as areas devoted to African tropical rainforest and temperate forest, and a superb cycad collection. Among the resident birds are African Finfoot, Purple-crested Turaco, Gorgeous Bush-shrike and Tambourine Dove, with Purple-banded Sunbird, Eastern Nicator and Green Twinspot among the other possibilities.

Harold Porter National Botanical Garden, Western Cape

Situated close to the seashore in Betty's Bay, and contiguous with the Kogelberg Biosphere Reserve, this magnificent garden has a superb collection of fynbos plants in cultivation, and footpaths through natural habitats leading up to Disa Falls. Forest patches of *Rapanea*, *Kiggelaria* and *Cunonia* are home to Cape Batis, Blue-mantled Crested Flycatcher, Sombre Greenbul and African Dusky Flycatcher, but the gardens are best known for the resident Victorin's Warbler (a rare South African endemic) that occurs in *Erica* and *Protea* scrub on the hillsides. Cape Rock Thrush, Cape Rockjumper and Ground Woodpecker occur on the higher slopes.

Walter Sisulu National Botanical Garden, Gauteng

Part of the Witwatersrand Ridge west of Johannesburg, this splendid garden conserves native highveld vegetation, with tall *Celtis*, *Combretum* and *Cussonia* trees as well as a wide variety of other South African plants on well laid-out paths and trails. This garden is well known for the magnificent Verreaux's Eagles that have nested alongside the Witpoortjie Falls for decades and are carefully monitored and vigorously protected by the local community. Other characteristic birds are Rock Kestrel, Brown-hooded Kingfisher, Red-throated Wryneck, Bokmakierie and Cape Rock Thrush.

Walter Sisulu National Botanical Garden

Pretoria National Botanical Garden, Gauteng

Situated on the northeastern edge of Pretoria, where the Magaliesberg reaches its eastern end, this garden features pristine *Burkea* and *Ochna* woodland along a central ridge. To the north there is a spectacular aloe and succulent collection, while various other South African plants, including some Cape flora, grow on the cooler southern slope. Birds of note include Crimson-breasted Shrike, Red-throated Wryneck, Brown-crowned Tchagra and Chinspot Batis, while the rare Ayres's Hawk Eagle is sometimes seen here.

KwaZulu-Natal National Botanical Garden, KwaZulu-Natal

Set in the western suburbs of Pietermaritzburg within a grassland area with pockets of kloof forest, this garden has a wide selection of South African plants, and there are several walking trails to explore. Among the resident birds are Red-fronted Tinkerbird, Bush Blackcap, Chorister Robin-chat, Purple-crested Turaco, Narina Trogon and Red-backed Mannikin, and Crowned Eagles are often also seen. This garden also has a wonderful diversity of dragonflies and butterflies.

Free State National Botanical Garden, Free State

Just north of Bloemfontein, set in a valley between dolerite koppies, this garden comprises grassy shrubland and open woodland dominated by impressive *Olea* and *Searsia* trees. A collection of frost-hardy South African plants, able to withstand cold winters, is under cultivation. Among the birds to be seen are Malachite Sunbird, African Red-eyed Bulbul, White-backed Mousebird, Karoo Thrush and Fairy Flycatcher.

Karoo Desert National Botanical Garden, Western Cape

Situated in Worcester in the Western Cape, this garden comprises natural shrubland and renosterbos. Succulent thickets with *heuweltjies* (strange but natural earth mounds) are a prominent feature of the landscape. The main visitors' area features a wide selection of plants from the semi-desert regions of South Africa. Among the birds that can be seen here are Ground Woodpecker, Cape Rock Thrush, Mountain Wheatear and Dusky Sunbird.

Botswana National Botanical Garden, Gaborone

Incorporating the Notwane River, and situated southeast of the capital city, this public garden is composed of six sections, each representative of a specific ecological region in Botswana. Native plants of cultural and medicinal importance – such as *Hoodia* and *Harpagophytum* – are under cultivation. Among the resident birds are Chestnut-vented Tit-babbler, White-browed Sparrow-weaver, Groundscraper Thrush and Violet-eared Waxbill. Southern White-faced Owls are sometimes seen.

Harold Porter National Botanical Garden

Namibia National Botanical Garden, Windhoek

This small garden is situated in the heart of the bustling capital city, with a selection of wonderful desert-adapted plants such as *Cyphostemma*, *Pachypodium* and *Euphorbia* under cultivation. A remarkable variety of birds has been recorded here, including Namibian endemics such as Damara Rockrunner, Damara Red-billed Hornbill, Monteiro's Hornbill and even the White-tailed Shrike. Pale-winged Starling, Crimson-breasted Shrike and Rosy-faced Lovebird are also present.

Zimbabwe National Botanical Garden, Harare

Situated in the suburb of Alexandra Park just north of Harare's CBD, this garden showcases indigenous plants from Zimbabwe's woodlands, including impressive *Brachystegia*, *Albizia* and *Afzelia* trees. Some parts of the garden are devoted to endangered species, and others to ornamental plants from India, South America and Australia. Among the exciting birds to be seen here are Whyte's Barbet, White-breasted Cuckooshrike and Purple-crested Turaco, with Red-throated Twinspot and Bat Hawk among the other possibilities.

Ewanrigg Botanical Garden, Harare

This wonderful garden is managed by Zimbabwe's National Parks and Wildlife Authority and situated about 30km northeast of the capital city. Ewanrigg has perhaps the largest and most impressive collection of aloes to be seen anywhere in the world and is best visited between April and July, when these succulent plants are in full bloom. The aloes provide a nectar feast for seven species of sunbird, including the rare Western Violet-backed Sunbird. A good variety of miombo birds are to be seen here, including the elusive Spotted Creeper.

USEFUL RESOURCES

MAGAZINES
African Birdlife
The bimonthly magazine *African Birdlife* (like its predecessor *Africa Birds & Birding*) is packed with fascinating articles and superb photography; anyone interested in birds should subscribe to this magazine and look out for back issues in second-hand stores. *African Birdlife* is the voice of BirdLife South Africa, a non-governmental body that campaigns for and implements conservation programmes; becoming a supporter of BirdLife is one of the best ways that you can help ensure that your grandchildren grow up in a country and a region that is still rich in birds and other wildlife.

WEB RESOURCES
There is no space here to list all of the useful websites relating to southern African birds, but the following are particularly recommended.

Animal Demography Unit (University of Cape Town): www.adu.uct.ac.za/
Coordinates bird ringing (SAFRING) and atlassing projects (SABAP2) in South Africa, and facilitates 'citizen science' in many areas.

Biodiversity Explorer: www.biodiversityexplorer.org/birds/
Excellent directory developed and maintained by the Natural History Collections Department of Iziko Museums of South Africa, with descriptions, photographs and distribution maps by various contributors; covers all wildlife, not only birds.

Ebedes Birds: www.ebedesbirds.co.za
Excellent photographic resource of southern African birds. Just go to the website and search for the species or family that interests you.

Invasive Species South Africa: www.invasives.org.za
A directory of invasive alien plants.

PlantZAfrica: www.plantzafrica.com
Excellent site maintained by the South African National Biodiversity Institute. Gives comprehensive information and photographs of plants, with tips on cultivation.

Trevor and Margaret Hardaker: Wildlife travels and photography in South Africa and abroad: www.hardaker.co.za
Excellent photographic resource of southern African birds.

Warwick Tarboton: www.warwicktarboton.co.za
A fabulous visual resource showcasing 40 years of this photographer's best images.

Xeno-Canto Foundation: www.xeno-canto.org
Unequalled resource for bird calls. Enthusiasts from all over the world contribute free recordings. You can listen to several different calls for each bird species (not always the case for commercially available bird call apps). Tells you exactly where each call was recorded.

SOCIAL MEDIA
Facebook and other social media are good ways to share your bird and wildlife sightings and are a source of information and inspiration. The following public groups are particularly useful:

For the Birds Ecological Garden: www.facebook.com/groups/birdsecogarden/

Wildlife in my Garden: www.facebook.com/groups/795997537085036/

LANDSCAPING
Many companies and individuals provide services to those who wish to landscape a wildlife garden, and you can find operators with the best track records in your area by asking your local nursery, searching the web or posing the question on your community Facebook group.

BirdLife South Africa
Isdell House, 17 Hume Road, Dunkeld West, Johannesburg, 2196
+27 (11) 789 1122
It is well worth visiting BirdLife's head office to see their inspiring, self-sustaining ecological garden.

EcoSolutions, Gauteng: www.ecosolutions.co.za
Provides and erects owl nesting boxes as well as providing solutions for management of rodent pests.

Grounded Landscaping: www.groundedlandscaping.co.za
Award-winning Johannesburg-based landscaping and garden designers specialising in indigenous gardens.

Kirstenbosch Garden Centre: www.sanbi.org/gardens/kirstenbosch/virtualtour/kirstenbosch-garden-centre
The best source for indigenous plants is often the closest national botanical garden. Kirstenbosch has a superb nursery, although most commercial nurseries now carry a good selection of native plants.

Witkoppen Wildflower Nursery: www.witkoppenwildflower.co.za
Just northwest of Fourways. This was South Africa's first indigenous plant nursery and continues to offer an extraordinary variety of trees, shrubs, bulbs, grasses and aquatic plants.

APPS AND ONLINE JOURNALS
A number of apps (online software programs) have been created as tools for bird-watchers.

Birdlasser: www.birdlasser.com
Local app in which you can record sightings, update your life list and, most importantly, make your observational data available to Southern Africa's Bird Atlassing Project (SABAP2).

Biological Observations: http://bo.adu.org.za/
Submit detailed observations of bird behaviour to this online journal produced by UCT's Animal Demography Unit.

eBird
Developed by Cornell Lab of Ornithology and the National Audubon Society in the USA, this global online checklist can be used anywhere, although the taxonomy (system of bird names) used differs slightly from that used in southern African lists.

Roberts VII Multimedia Birds of Southern Africa: Apple store/Google Play
Digital version of the illustrated *Roberts Birds VII*. Includes bird calls and other content. Allows the user to create bird lists and tap into current data.

Sasol eBirds: Apple store/Google Play/Blackberry World/Windows Phone Store
Digital version of the illustrated *Sasol Birds of Southern Africa*. Includes bird calls and other content. Allows the user to create bird lists and tap into current data.

BIRD RESCUE

Fledgling owls found on the ground do not need to be 'rescued', but if you should find an injured adult owl or other bird of prey then contact one of these non-profit organisations.

Owl Rescue Centre, Gauteng: www.owlrescue911.webs.com / 082 719 5463

Eagle Encounters, Western Cape: www.eagle-encounters.co.za / +27 (21) 858 1826

REFERENCES & FURTHER READING

BIRDS

Chittenden, H., Allan, D. & Weiersbye, I. 2012. *Roberts Geographic Variation of Southern African Birds*. John Voelcker Bird Book Fund, Cape Town.

Chittenden, H., Davies, R. & Weiersbye, I. 2016. *Roberts Bird Guide*. John Voelcker Bird Book Fund, Cape Town.

Cocker, M. & Tipling, D. 2013. *Birds and People*. Jonathan Cape, London.

Cohen, C., Spottiswoode, C & Rossouw, J. 2006. *Southern African Birdfinder: Where to Find 1,400 Bird Species in Southern Africa and Madagascar*. Struik, Cape Town.

Hancock, P. & Weiersbye, I. 2016. *Birds of Botswana*. Princeton University Press, New Jersey.

Hockey, P.A.R., Dean, W.R.J. & Ryan, P.G. (Eds). 2005. *Roberts Birds of Southern Africa*. 7th edition. John Voelcker Bird Book Fund, Cape Town.

Irwin, M.P.S. 1981. *Birds of Zimbabwe*. Quest, Salisbury.

Loon, R. & H. 2005. *Birds – the Inside Story: Exploring Birds and their Behaviour in Southern Africa*. Struik, Cape Town.

Newman, K. & Newman, V. 2010. *Newman's Birds of Southern Africa*. Struik Nature, Cape Town.

Peacock, F. 2012. *Chamberlain's LBJs: the Definitive Guide to Southern Africa's Little Brown Jobs*. Mirafra, Pretoria.

Ryan, P. 2008. *Kirstenbosch Birds & Other WIldlife*. Struik Nature, Cape Town.

Sinclair, I. 2017. *Pocket Guide Birds of Namibia*. Struik Nature, Cape Town.

Sinclair, I., Hockey, P., Tarboton, W. & Ryan, P. 2011. *Sasol Birds of Southern Africa*. Struik Nature, Cape Town.

Skutch, A.F. 1975. *Parent Birds and Their Young*. University of Texas Press, Houston.

Steyn, P. 1996. *Nesting Birds: the Breeding Habits of Southern African Birds*. Fernwood Press, Cape Town.

Tarboton, W. 2011. *Roberts Nests and Eggs of southern African Birds*. John Voelcker Bird Book Fund, Cape Town.

Taylor, M., Peacock, F. & Wanless, R.M. 2015. *The 2015 Eskom Red Data Book of Birds of South Africa, Lesotho and Swaziland*. BirdLife South Africa, Dunkeld West.

PLANTS

Burrows, J. & Burrows, S. 2003. *Figs of Southern and South-Central Africa*. Umdaus, Pretoria.

Coates-Palgrave, M. 2002. *Trees of Southern Africa*. Struik, Cape Town.

Ebedes, G. 2017. *Gardener's Guide Indigenous Garden Plants of southern Africa*. Struik Nature, Cape Town.

Glen, H. & Van Wyk, B. 2016. *Guide to Trees Introduced into Southern Africa*. Struik Nature, Cape Town.

Johnson, D. & S. 1993. *Gardening with Indigenous Trees and Shrubs*. Southern Book Publishers, Halfway House.

Manning, J. 2007. *Field Guide to Fynbos*. Struik, Cape Town.

Manning, J. 2009. *Field Guide to Wild Flowers of South Africa*. Struik Nature, Cape Town.

Pooley, E. 2006. *Forest Plants in the Forest and in the Garden*. Flora and Fauna Publications, Durban.

Schmidt, E., Lotter, M. & McCleland, W. 2002. *Trees and Shrubs of Mpumalanga and Kruger National Park*. Jacana, Johannesburg.

Van Wyk, B. & Van Wyk, P. 2013. *Field Guide to Trees of Southern Africa*. Struik Nature, Cape Town.

OTHER FAUNA

Alexander, G. & Marais, J. 2007. *A Guide to the Reptiles of Southern Africa*. Struik, Cape Town.

Botha, C. & J. 2010. *Bring Nature Back To Your Garden*. Flora and Fauna Publications Trust, Durban.

Butchart, D. 2009. *Wildlife of South Africa: A Photographic Guide*. Struik Nature, Cape Town.

Carruthers, V. (Ed.). 2016. *Wildlife of Southern Africa*. Struik Nature, Cape Town.

Du Preez, L. & Carruthers, V. 2017. *Frogs of Southern Africa: A Complete Guide*. Struik Nature, Cape Town.

Durrell, G. & L. 1993. *The Amateur Naturalist*. Dorling Kindersley, London.

Holm, E. 2017. *Insectlopedia*. Struik Nature, Cape Town.

Ledger, J.A. (Ed.). 1979. *African Insect Life: S.H. Skaife*. Struik, Cape Town.

Picker, M. & Griffiths, C. 2011. *Alien and Invasive Animals: a South African perspective*. Struik Nature, Cape Town.

Woodhall, S. & Gray, L. 2015. *Gardening for Butterflies: Planning and Planting an Insect-friendly Garden in South Africa*. Struik Nature, Cape Town.

Woodhall, S. 2005. *Field Guide to Butterflies of South Africa*. Struik Nature, Cape Town.

Tarboton, W. & M. 2015. *A Guide to the Dragonflies and Damselflies of South Africa*. Struik Nature, Cape Town.

GLOSSARY

Alien a species occurring outside of its natural range; deliberately or accidentally introduced by humans
Allopreening Mutual preening to strengthen a pair bond
Arboreal tree-living
Brooding the process whereby parent birds keep their nestlings warm in the nest
Cere a raised, fleshy area at the base of the upper bill
Clutch a set of eggs
Colonial birds that nest close to one another in a tight or loose cluster
Cooperative breeding when non-parental adults (typically offspring from a previous brood) assist the breeding pair in the feeding of young
Cryptic camouflaged coloration
Dimorphic sexes occurring in two distinct forms that may differ in plumage, size or other features
Display a ritualised signal or series of movements that conveys a specific message
Eclipse plumage a brief phase of drab, female-like plumage in male birds at the end of a breeding cycle (e.g. in the Malachite Sunbird)
Feral a non-native species with a self-sustaining population
Fledging the process of developing feathers and preparing to leave the nest
Fledgling a young bird that has left the nest but is still dependent on parental feeding
Gape the opening created when the bill/mouth is fully open; also used to describe the brightly coloured fleshy corners of the bill in nestlings and fledglings
Gorget a necklace-like throat marking (e.g. that of the Bokmakierie)
Host a bird in whose nest a cuckoo or other brood parasite deposits its eggs; the host then provides parental care in the belief that it is raising its own young
Immature a young bird no longer under parental care that has moulted from juvenile plumage but has not acquired adult plumage
Irruption a sudden movement of large numbers of a bird species into an area where they are typically rare or even unknown
Jizz (Giss) the general impression, shape and size that a particular bird species gives when perched, moving or in flight; used by experienced birders who have come to recognise subtleties that others might overlook or miss
Juvenile a bird in its first feathered plumage; in most songbirds this stage is very short and juvenile feathers are replaced within a few weeks of leaving the nest, but larger raptors and some others may retain juvenile plumage for a full year
Malar stripe line from base of bill down the throat
Mantle feathered area from the centre of the back to the back of the neck

Migrant a bird that undertakes predictable annual movements
Mobbing the harassment of an owl, snake, cat or other predator by a group of birds intent on driving it out of their immediate vicinity
Montane living in mountainous country
Nape feathered area at the back of the head
Niche a specialised ecological role or function
Nocturnal active after dark
Nomadic making erratic movements, often in response to rainfall
Non-breeding plumage an extended phase of drab plumage in male birds (e.g. bishops and widows)
Palearctic zoogeographic region of Europe and northern Asia (also includes North Africa)
Passerine a member of the order Passeriformes, which includes more than half of all bird species; all passerines have three forward-facing toes and one that faces backwards; they also have control over their syrinx muscles, which allows many species to produce a wide range of songs, often musical to the human ear
Pellet a mass of indigestible material such as beetle wing cases, fur, feathers and bones regurgitated by owls, herons, kingfishers and some other birds; can be picked apart and analysed to determine diet
Polyandry breeding relationship in which one female reproduces with two or more males, simultaneously (e.g. African Jacana and Painted Snipe, where males perform incubating and brooding)
Polygyny breeding relationship in which one male reproduces with two or more females, simultaneously (e.g. weavers, bishops, whydahs)
Precocial describing young that are fairly mature from birth
Race another name for a subspecies
Resident a bird that remains in the same general area throughout the year, not undertaking any migration or other movement
Rump feathered area above the tail
Scrape nest little more than a shallow depression in which camouflaged eggs are laid (e.g. thick-knees and plovers)
Songbird a passerine, see above
Species a division within a genus that may contain one or more subspecies (races)
Subspecies a geographical division of a species, showing differences in morphology, coloration or voice when compared with other members of the species, but able to interbreed with them in border areas (e.g. Bar-throated Apalis has 13 subspecies in southern Africa)
Supercillium the area above the eye ('eyebrow')
Syrinx the filamentous structure at the base of the trachea ('windpipe') through which a bird produces vocalisations
Terrestrial ground-living
Vagrant a bird that appears in a locality beyond its normal range (a stray)
Vent feathered area between the legs where the tail feathers begin
Wattle bare, fleshy skin around the eyes, base of bill or throat

INDEXES

This index covers common and scientific names of bird and plant species only. Numbers in **bold** refer to photographs.

INDEX TO BIRD NAMES

Accipiter tachiro 57
Acridotheres tristis 118
Alopochen aegyptiaca 54
Amadina erythrocephala 137
Amblyospiza albifrons 141
Andropadus importunus 103
Apalis thoracica 97
Apalis, Bar-throated 97
   Yellow-breasted 97
apalises 16, 20, 96, 97, 158
Apus 83
Apus caffer 82
Babbler, Arrow-marked 110
   Southern Pied 110
Barbet, Acacia Pied 76
   Black-collared 41, 74
   Crested 30, 33, 75
   White-eared 74
   Whyte's 74, 185
barbets 20, 30, 31, 34, 36, 74, **74**, 75, 76, 118, 134, 158, 159, 161, 162, 165, 166, 168, 169, 171, 172
barn owls 35
Batis capensis 95
Batis, Cape 95, 182, 183
   Chinspot 95, 184
batises 45, 95, 162
bee-eaters 27
Bishop, Southern Red 143
bishops 19, 143
Blackcap, Bush 184
   Eurasian 153
Bokmakierie 31, 114, 183
Bostrychia hagedash 51
Boubou, Southern 46, 48, 115
   Tropical 115
boubous 16, 29, 31, 115
Brownbul, Terrestrial 103
Brubru 116
Bubo africanus 68
Bulbul, African Red-eyed 100, 101, 102, 184
   Cape 44, 46, 100, 101
   Dark-capped 100, 101, 102
bulbuls 16, 20, 30, 31, 33, 44, 96, **100**, 101, 102, 158, 162, 165, 166, 168, 169, 171, 172, 176, 181
Bunting, Lark-like 151
Burhinus capensis 55
Bush-shrike, Gorgeous 183
   Grey-headed 114
   Orange-breasted 114
bush-shrikes 31, 33, 94, 114

Butcher Bird see Fiscal, Southern
Buzzard, Common 56
Bycanistes bucinator 71
Camaroptera, Green-backed 98
canaries 17, 19, 23, 29, **148**, 149, 150, 160, 161, 164
Canary, Atlantic 148
   Brimstone 29, **45**, 150, 169
   Bully see Canary, Brimstone
   Cape 149
   Yellow 148, 150
   Yellow-fronted 148
Cecropis abyssinica 85
   C. cucullata 84
Centropus burchellii 62
Cercomela familiaris 108
Chalcomitra amethystine 129
   C. senegalensis 128
Chat, Familiar 30, 108
   Mocking Cliff 107
Chrysococcyx caprius 67
Cinnyricinclus leucogaster 120
Cinnyris chalybeus 127
   C. talatala 126
Colius striatus 81
Columba guinea 58
Corythaixoides concolor 63
Cossypha caffra 111
   C. heuglini 113
   C. natalensis 112
Coucal, Burchell's 43, 62
   Senegal 62
coucals 16, 24, 30, 62
Crake, Spotted 153
Creeper, Spotted 185
Crithagra gularis 151
   C. mozambicus 148
   C. sulphuratus 150
Crombec, Long-billed 160
Cuckoo, Black 115
   Common 66
   Diederik 67, 96, 133, 138, 139, 143, 163
   Great Spotted 121, 122, **123**
   Jacobin 100, 102, 103
   Klaas's 67, 95, 96, 125, 130
   Levaillant's 110
   Red-chested 36, 47, 66, 67, 104, 105, 109, 111, 113, 162, 163
cuckoos 16, 66, 67, 123, 162
Cuckooshrike, Black 89
   White-breasted 185
Cuculus canorus 66
   C. solitarius 66
Cypsiurus parvus 83

Dendropicos fuscescens 78
Dicrurus adsimilis 88
dikkop see thick-knees
Dove, African Mourning 60
   Cape Turtle 61
   Laughing 59
   Lemon 61, 182
   Namaqua 59
   Red-eyed 60
   Tambourine 39, 183
doves 23, 24, 29, 33, 38, 44, **59**, 60, 61
Drongo, Fork-tailed 43, **88**, 89
   Square-tailed 88
drongos 17, 30, 31, 45, 88, 161
Dryoscopus cubla 116
Duck, Yellow-billed 54
eagle-owls 35
Eagle, Ayres's Hawk 184
   Crowned 153, 184
   Verreaux's 183
egrets 26
Estrilda astrild 147
Euplectes orix 143
Finch, Cut-throat 137
   Red-headed 137
   Scaly-feathered 49, **136**
finches 29, 136, 137, 145
Finfoot, African 183
firefinches 42
Fiscal, Southern 46, 93, 117
Flufftail, Buff-spotted 153
flufftails 38
Flycatcher, African Dusky 47, 90, 91, 92, 183
   African Paradise 16, 26, 45, **94**, 162
   Ashy 50, 91, 92
   Blue-grey see Flycatcher, Ashy
   Blue-mantled Crested 94, 183
   Collared 153
   Fairy 184
   Fiscal 15, 93, 117
   Marico 92
   Southern Black 89
   Spotted 47, 90, 91, 92
flycatchers 17, 20, 27, 30, 31, 34, 45, 78, **89**, 90, 91, 92, 93, 94, 116, 158, 162, 165, 179
geese 54
Go-away-bird, Grey 28, 30, **63**, 167, 181
Goose, Egyptian 54
Goshawk, African 30, 33, 57

goshawks 24, 38, 56, **57**, 94
Grassbird, African 182
Greenbul, Sombre 103, 183
greenbuls 103, 162
Guineafowl, Crested 52
   Helmeted 52
Gymnogene see Hawk, African Harrier-
Halcyon albiventris 79
Hamerkop **26**, 69
harriers 56
Hawk, African Harrier- 56
   Bat 185
Hedydipna collaris 130
herons 26, 31
hirundines 47
Hirundo fuligula 87
   H. rustica 86
Honeyguide, Greater 120, 121
   Lesser 74, 76, 77, 120, 134
Hoopoe, African 72
hoopoes 19, 20, 34, 45, **72**
Hornbill, African Grey 70
   Crowned 71
   Damara Red-billed 185
   Monteiro's 70, 185
   Southern Red-billed 70
   Southern Yellow-billed 70
   Trumpeter 71
hornbills 70, 71, 162
Hummingbird, Bee 42
hummingbirds 32
Ibis, African Sacred 51
   Glossy 51
   Hadeda 33, 51
   Southern Bald 51
Indigobird, Village 142
Jacky Hangman see Fiscal, Southern
Jynx ruficollis 77
   J. torquilla 77
Kestrel, Rock 183
Kingfisher, African Pygmy 38, **38**
   Brown-hooded 26, 38, **79**, 183
   Malachite 26
   Woodland 79
kingfishers 19, 25, 26, 31, 34, 38, 45, 79
Kite, Yellow-billed 56
Lamprotornis nitens 121
Laniarius ferrugineus 115
Lanius collaris 117
Lonchura cucullata 144

189

Lophoceros nasutus 70
Lourie, Knysna see
 Turaco, Knysna
Lovebird, Rosy-faced 185
Lybius torquatus 74

Mallard 54
Mannikin, Bronze 29, **144**
 Red-backed 144, 184
mannikins 17, 19, 33, **144**
Martin, Brown-throated 87
 Rock 87
martins 33, 87, 166
Melaenornis pammelaina 89
Motacilla capensis 109
Mousebird, Red-faced 80
 Speckled 27, 28, 80, 81
 White-backed 29, 80, 81, 184
mousebirds 16, 33, 27, 45, 80, 81, 93, 162, 166, 171, 172, 181
Muscicapa adusta 91
 M. caerulescens 92
 M. striata 90
Myna, Common 118

Nectarinia famosa 125, 127
Nicator, Eastern 183
nightjars 26, 31
Numida meleagris 52

Onychognathus morio 122
Oriole, Black-headed 99, 161
 Eurasian Golden 99
orioles 16, 99, 161, 173, 176
Oriolus larvatus 99
Ostrich, Common 42
Owl, African Wood 34, 35, 69, 182
 Cape Eagle- 68
 Pel's Fishing 153
 Southern White-faced 184
 Spotted Eagle- 34, 35, 46, 49, 54, **68**, 182
 Verreaux's Eagle- 68
 Western Barn 34, **69**
Owlet, Pearl-spotted 88
owlets 34
owls 31, 34, **35**, 36, **68**, 69, 94, 168

parrots 161
Passer diffusus 134
 P. domesticus 132
 P. melanurus 133
Penduline-tit, Cape 42
Phoeniculus purpureus 73
Phylloscopus trochilus 98
Pigeon, African Green 20, 58
 African Olive 58, 166
 Rock 58
 Speckled 58
pigeons 58, 162, 172, 181
Pitta, African 152

Plocepasser mahali 135
Ploceus capensis 140
 P. cucullatus 138
 P. velatus 139
Polyboroides typus 56
Prinia maculosa 96
Prinia, Black-chested 96
 Karoo 43, 96
 Tawny-flanked 96
Promerops cafer 124
Pternistes capensis 53
Puffback, Black-backed **116**, 160
Pycnonotus capensis 101
 P. nigricans 100
 P. tricolor 102
Pytilia, Green-winged 146

Quelea quelea 142
Quelea, Red-billed 142

Robin-chat, Cape 8, 22, 46, 49, 66, **111**, 112, 113
 Chorister 112, 184
 Red-capped 47, 111, **112**
 White-browed 8, 34, 45, 111, **113**
robin-chats 16, 20, 27, 29, 30, 31, 93, **111**, 112, 113, 167
Robin, Heuglin's see Robin-chat, White-browed
 Natal see Robin-chat, Red-capped
 Rufous-tailed 153
Rockjumper, Cape 183
Rockrunner, Damara 185
rollers 34

Scimitarbill, Common 73
Secretarybird 56
Seedeater, Streaky-headed 151
Serinus canaria 148
 S. canicollis 149
Shikra 57
Shrike, Crimson-breasted 184, 185
 White-tailed 185
shrikes 30, 31, 176
Sigelus silens 93
Siskin, Cape 182
Sparrow-weaver, White-browed **135**, 184
Sparrow, Cape 28, 29, **133**, 134
 Great 132
 House 28, **132**, 134
 Southern Grey-headed 134
Sparrowhawk, Black 57
 Little 57
 Ovambo 57
sparrowhawks 24, 38
sparrows 27, 29, 33, 38, 44, **132**, **133**, **134**, 135, 136, 159
Spekvreter see Chat, Familiar
Sporopipes squamifrons 136

Spreo bicolor 123
Spurfowl, Cape 53, 166
 Natal 53
 Red-billed 53
spurfowls 29, **53**
Starling, Burchell's 121
 Cape Glossy 121, 161, **177**
 Common 118, **119**
 Greater Blue-eared 121
 Pale-winged 122, 185
 Pied 123
 Red-winged 122
 Violet-backed 44, 47, **120**
starlings 20, 30, 34, 44, 119, **120**, 121, 122, 123, 158, 161, 165, 166, 168, 169, 171, 173, 176, 181
Streptopelia capicola 61
 S. semitorquata 60
 S. senegalensis 59
Strigidae 69
Sturnus vulgaris 119
Sugarbird, Cape 29, 33, 49, 102, **124**, 182
 Gurney's 124
sugarbirds **124**, 174
Sunbird, Amethyst 128, **129**
 Collared 130
 Dusky 184
 Greater Double-collared 127
 Malachite 46, **125**, 127, 182, 184
 Marico 126
 Orange-breasted 182
 Purple-banded 183
 Scarlet-chested 128, 129, 176
 Southern Double-collared 127
 Variable 130
 Western Violet-backed 185
 White-bellied 126
sunbirds 17, 32, 33, 45, 93, 124, **125**, **126**, **127**, **128**, **129**, **130**, 160, 161, 164, 166, 170, 173, 174, 176, 185
Swallow, Barn 47, **86**
 Greater Striped 47, **47**, 84, 85
 Lesser Striped 84, **85**
 South African Cliff 87
 White-throated 86
swallows 20, 26, 31, 33, 47, 82, **84**, **85**, **86**, 166
Swift, African Palm 83
 Bradfield's 83
 Little 82
 White-rumped 82, 84, 85
swifts 26, 47, **82**, **83**, 166

Tchagra, Brown-crowned 184
Telophorus zeylonus 114
Terpsiphone viridis 94
Thamnolaea cinnamomeiventris 107

Thick-knee, Spotted 15, 45, **55**
 Water 55
thick-knees 31, **55**
Thrush, Cape Rock 107, 183, 184
 Groundscraper 106, 184
 Karoo 23, 66, **104**, 105, 106, 184
 Kurrichane 106
 Olive 104, **105**, 106
thrushes 16, 20, 25, 31, 37, **104**, **105**, **106**, 158, 165, 169, 171
Tinkerbird, Red-fronted 76, 184
 Yellow-fronted 76
tinkerbirds 162
Tit-babbler, Chestnut-vented 184
Tit, Southern Black 160
tits 34, 78, **160**, 161
Trachyphonus vaillantii 75
Tricholaema leucomelas 76
Trogon, Narina 152, 184
trogons 153
Tuaraco corythaix 64, 65
 T. porphyreolophus 64
Turaco, Knysna 64, **65**
 Livingstone's 65
 Purple-crested 23, **64**, 183, 184, 185
turacos **64**, **65**, 158, 162, 169
Turdoides jardinii 110
Turdus libonyanus 106
 T. olivaceus 105
 T. smithii 104
Twinspot, Green 153, 183
 Red-throated 185
twinspots 38, 153
Tyto alba 69
Tytonidae 69

Upupa africana 72
Uraeginthus angolensis 146
Urocolius indicus 80

Vidua macroura 145

Wagtail, African Pied 109
 Cape 18, **18**, 66, 109
wagtails 27, **109**
Warbler, Garden 98
 Icterine 98
 Victorin's 183
 Willow 47, **98**
warblers 16, 45, **98**, 158, 167
Waxbill, Blue 146, 180
 Common 23, 29, 145, **147**
 Swee 147
 Violet-eared 184
waxbills 17, 19, 23, 29, 33, 42, 136, **146**, **147**
Weaver, African (Holub's) Golden 140
 Cape 28, 32, 139, **140**
 Lesser Masked 139

Sociable **29**, **136**
Southern Masked 138, **139**, 140
Spotted-backed see Weaver, Village
Thick-billed **29**, **141**, 162
Village **138**, **139**
weavers 19, 32, 33, 44, **67**, **136**, **138**, **139**, **140**, **141**, 143, 159, 161, 174, 176
Wheatear, Mountain **108**, 184
White-eye, African Yellow 131
Cape **20**, **40**, **49**, **131**, 161
Orange River 131
white-eyes 16, 20, 27, 30, 32, 33, 116, 126, **131**, 158, 161, 162, 165, 166, 168, 170, 171, 172, 173, 176
Whydah, Pin-tailed 142, 144, **145**, 147
Shaft-tailed 145, 146
Wood-hoopoe, Green **73**, 159
wood-hoopoes **73**, 160, 167
Woodpecker, Cardinal **78**, 160
Golden-tailed **78**
Ground 183, 184
Olive **77**
woodpeckers 16, 34, 45, **77**, **78**, 95, 134, 159, 160, 161
Wryneck, Eurasian 77
Red-throated **77**, 183, 184
wrynecks 34, **77**

***Z**osterops capensis* **131**

INDEX TO PLANT NAMES

Acacia 76, 116
A. cyclops 122, **181**
acacias 156
Acrocarpus 99, 126, 129
Afzelia 185
A. quanzensis 71
Agapanthus **179**
Agapanthus praecox **179**
Agave 76, 88, 126, 127
A. sisalina 176
Albizia 130, 185
A. adianthifolia **160**
A. versicolor **160**
Albizia, Largeleaf **160**
Aloe 32, 73, 74, 76, 88, 99, 100, 101, 102, 107, 121, 122, 124, 125, 126, 127, 128, 129, 130, 131, 138, 151
A. arborescens 129, **177**
A. castanea 177
A. chabaudii 177
A. chabaudii 128, **176**, 177
A. ferox 177
A. lutescens 177
A. marlothii **177**

A. pluridens 177
A. rupestris 177
A. striata 177
A. thraskii **176**, 177
Aloe, Bitter 177
Bottlebrush 177
Cattail 177
Coral 177
Dune **40**, **176**, 177
French 177
Krantz **177**
Mountain **177**
Spear 177
Swazi **176**, 177
aloes 17, **17**, 176, **176**, 184, 185
Alternanthera pungens 134
Anthocleista 64
A. grandiflora **158**
Antidesma 64, 91, 92, 102, 103, 106, 120, 131
A. venosum **158**
Apodytes 120
A. dimidiata **169**
Ash, Cape 80, 162
Asparagus 97, 112
Asphodelaceae 176

Banana, Wild 173
Baobab 12, 156
Bauhinia galpinii **164**
Beech, Cape 172
Berchemia 71, 103, 120
B. discolor **169**
Bigleaf Tree **158**
Boerbean, Weeping **161**
Borassus 83
Boscia 76, 100, 120
Bottlebrush, Weeping 124
Brachystegia 185
Bramble 181
Bridelia micrantha **170**
Brunsvigia 175
Buddleja saliviifolia 149, **165**
Buffalo Thorn 156, **167**
Bugweed 181
bulbines 176
bulrushes 25, 27, **27**
Burchellia 130
Burkea 184
Bushwillow, Forest 13
River **164**

Cabbage Tree, Common **159**
Callistemon 125, 126, 127, 129
C. viminalis 124
Calpurnia aurea **173**
Camphor Tree **165**
Camphor, Wild 150
Carissa 101
C. macrocarpa 16, **167**

Celtis 104, 116, 183
C. africana 33, 141, **154**, 162
Chaetacme aristata 141
Cheesewood 172
Christmas Tree, New Zealand 124
Chrysanthemoides 53, 80, 81, 101
C. monilifera **166**
Clivia 64, 65
C. miniata **179**
Combretum 116, 130, 148, 164, 183
C. erythrophyllum **164**
C. microphyllum 130, **164**
Commiphora 17, 70, 107, 120
Coral Tree, Coastal **161**
Sacred **161**
Cotoneaster **181**
Cotoneaster 181
Crowberry, Dune **171**
Cunonia 183
Cussonia 74, 122, 183
C. paniculata **159**
C. spicata **159**
cycads 71
Cynodon dactylon 19
Cyphostemma **185**

Dactyloctenium australe 19
Dagga, Wild 156, **173**
Deurmekaarbos see Puzzlebush
Diospyros 63, 74
Dodonea 16
Dombeya rotundifolia **163**
Dovyalis 76
Dracaena 112

Ehretia rigida **169**
Eichhornia crassipes 25
Ekebergia 65, 70, 71, 75, 80, 81, 103
E. capensis 80, **162**
Elm, Thorny 141
Erica 13, 127, 149, 183
E. perspicua **175**
ericas 17
Eriobotrya japonica 181
Eriocephalus 96, 97, 149
Erythrina 73, 74, 99, 121, 122, 126, 127, 128, 129, 131, **138**, 148, 151
E. caffra **161**
E. lysistemon **161**
Eucalyptus 88, 99, 123, 126
Euclea 13, 16, 63, 76
Euphorbia 13, 185
euphorbias 17
Fever Tree 16, 33, **159**
Ficus 70, 71, 80, 81, 120
F. natalensis **20**, **168**
F. sur **21**, **168**
F. sycomorus 20

Fig, Broom Cluster **21**, **168**
Natal Strangler **168**
Strangler **20**
Sycamore **20**
Firethorn 181
Yellow 131
Flame Creeper 130, **164**
Flatcrown **160**

Gladiolus 175
Grass, Broad-leaved Bristle 19, **180**
Buffalo 19
Guinea 19
Kikuyu 18
Kweek 19
L.M. 19
Natal Redtop 19
grasses **19**, 180
Grevillea 99, 121, 125, 126
Guava 181
Gymnosporea 60

Halleria 75, 93, 126, 127, 129, 130
H. lucida 126, **166**
Harpagophytum 184
Harpephyllum 64
H. caffrum **65**, **163**
Heath, Prince-of-Wales **175**
Helianthus annuus 141
Holly, Cape 172
Honeysuckle, Cape 170
Hoodia 184
Hyacinth, Water 25
Hyphaene 83
Hypoestes aristata **179**

Ilex mitis 172
Ivory, Brown **169**

Jambolan 181

Karee **171**
Keurboom **170**
Kigelia 128, 129
K. africana 130
Kiggelaria 75, 101, 104, 122, 131, 183
K. africana 66, 67, 141, **163**
Kirkia 17
Kniphofia 19, 125, 129
Knobthorn 12

Laburnum, Wild **173**
Lantana 181
Lantana 61, 102, 103, 151
L. camara 181
Lavandula spica 149
Lavender 149
Leadwood 12
Leonotis 125, 126, 127, 128
L. leonurus **173**
Leptospermum laevigatum 181

Lettuce, Water 25
Leucospermum 124
   L. cordifolium **174**
lichen 97
Ligustrum 181
Lily, Bush **179**
   Guernsey **155**
Loquat 181
Loranthus 76
Lycium 134

Mahogany, Natal **168**
Marula 12, 156
Melia 80, 81
   M. azederach 63, 122, 141, **181**
Melinis repens 19
Metrosideros 125
   M. excelsa 124
Milkwood, White 86, **166**
Mimetes 124
   M. hirtus **175**
Mitzeerie **170**
Monkey Thorn, Black 33
Mopane 12, 156
Morus 80, 81, 91, 118, 151, 181
   M. nigra 63
moss 97
Mulberry 63, 181
Myrtle, Australian 181

Nerine 175
   N. samiensis **155**
Nicotiniana 127
Numnum, Big **167**

Oaks 34
Ochna 90, 184
Olea 184
Opuntia 151
   O. robusta 181
Oxalis 149

Pachypodium 185
Pagoda, Marsh **175**
Palm Tree **83**
Panicum maximum 19
Paperbark Thorn 159
Paperthorn 134
Pappea capensis **165**
Passiflora 181
Passion Fruits 181
Peach, Wild 66, 67, 141, 156, **163**
Pear, Hard 13
   Prickly 181
   White **169**
   Wild **163**
Pennisetum clandestinum 18
Pepper Tree, Brazilian 100, 131, 181
Phragmites 141
Phyllanthus 103, 106, 120
   P. reticulatus **171**
Pigeonwood **162**
Pincushion 124, **174**
pines 156
Pistia stratiotes 25
Pittosporum 65
   P. viridiflorum **172**
Plectranthus 17, 178
Plum, Bird see Ivory, Brown
   Jacket **165**
   Wild 65, **163**
Portulacaria 13
Potato Bush **171**
Potato Creeper 181
Pride of De Kaap **164**
Privet 181
Protea 13, 124, 125, 150, 151, 183
   P. cynaroides **175**
   P. repens **174**
   P. susannae **174**
Protea, King **175**
Psidium guajava 181
Puzzlebush **169**
Pyracantha 61, 80, 81, 118, 119, 181
   P. angustifolia 131

Rapanea 183
   R. melanophloeos **172**
Rauvolfia 71
red-hot pokers 176
restios 175
Ribbonbush **179**
Rubus 181

Sagewood 149, **165**
Salvia 96, 101, 127
Sausage Tree 130
Scadoxis 112
Schinus molle 100, 131
   S. terebinthifolius 181
Schotia 74, 99, 102, 121, 126, 128, 138, 151
   S. brachypetala **161**
Searsia 16, 61, 76, 80, 81, 96, 97, 100, 101, 103, 134, 184
   S. (Rhus) crenata **171**
   S. (Rhus) lancea **171**
Senegalia 156
   S. mellifera 33
Setaria megaphylla 19, **180**
Sideroxylon 65, 74
   S. inerme 86, **166**
Sisal 176
Solanum 102, 103
   S. mauritianum 181
   S. seaforthianum 181
Stenotaphrum secundatum 19
Stinkwood, White 13, 33, 141, **154**, **162**
Strelitzia 129, 130, 131
   S. nicolai **173**
   S. regina **173**
succulents 184
Sugarbush **174**
   Stink-leaf **174**
Sunflower 141
Sweet Thorn 33, **160**
Syringa 63, 141, **181**

Syzygium 74
   S. cordatum **167**
   S. cumini 181

Tapinanthus 80, 81, 126, 128
Tarchonanthus 96, 97
   T. camphoratus **165**
   T. littoralis 150, **165**
Tasselberry **158**
Tecoma 125, 126, 129, 151
   T. (Tecomaria) capensis **170**
Tecomaria 32
Tickberry, Bush **166**
Tree Fuchsia 126, **166**
Trema 60, 90, 91, 92, 102, 106, 112, 131
   T. orientalis **162**
Trichelia 64, 71
   T. emetica **168**
Typha 141

Vachellia 156
   V. (Acacia) karroo 33, **160**
   V. (Acacia) sieberiana **159**
   V. (Acacia) xanthophloea 33, **159**
Vepris 91
Virgilia oroboides **170**
Viscum 76

Wachendorfia 19
Washingtonia **83**
water lilies 25
Waterberry **167**
Watsonia 125, 175
Wattle, Red-eye **181**
wattles 156
willows 34

Yellowwood 13

Ziziphus 63
   Z. mucronata **167**